ALL ONE BODY WE

ALL ONE BODY WE

The Doctrine of the Church in Ecumenical Perspective

by

JOHN H. KROMMINGA

President
Calvin Theological Seminary

WILLIAM B. EERDMANS PUBLISHING COMPANY
GRAND RAPIDS, MICHIGAN

Library of Congress Catalog Card Number: 76-120844
Printed in the United States of America

Permissions to quote from the following named publications are acknowledged as follows:

from *The World Council of Churches* by David P. Gaines: copyright 1966 by David P. Gaines. William L. Bauhan, Publisher, Peterborough, N.H. 03458;

from *The Ecumenical Review*: The World Council of Churches and *The Ecumenical Review;*

from *The Nature of the Church* by R. Newton Flew (ed.), 1952, and *The Evanston Report* by W. A. Visser 't Hooft, 1955: Harper & Row;

from *The Churches and the Church* by Bernard Leeming: copyright © 1960, Bernard Leeming, S.J.;

from *The Church* (New Directions in Theology Today, Volume IV), by Colin W. Williams: Copyright C MCMLXVIII, The Westminster Press, used by permission;

from *Institutionalism and Church Unity* by Nils Ehrenstrom and Walter Muelder (eds.), 1963, and *The New Delhi Report* by Visser 't Hooft, 1962: The World Council of Churches and Association Press;

from *A Documentary History of the Faith and Order Movement* by Lukas Vischer, 1963: The World Council of Churches and Bethany Press;

from *The Uppsala Report 1968* by Norman Goodall (ed.), 1968, and *New Delhi to Uppsala* and *Drafts for Sections,* both by WCC, 1968: The World Council of Churches.

CONTENTS

ACKNOWLEDGMENTS

This study is the fruit of a sabbatical year spent in Cambridge, England, 1968-69. My hearty appreciation is expressed to certain parties who made this effort possible. My thanks first of all to the Board of Trustees of Calvin College and Seminary, who offered a sabbatical to one who was seeking to be a part-time teacher as well as a full-time administrator. My thanks also to the Faculty Fellowship Fund of the American Association of Theological Schools, for a study grant that opened the door still farther. Thanks to Fitzwilliam College and Cambridge University for library privileges. My warm appreciation is extended also to Principal McLeod and all the others at Westminster and Cheshunt Colleges in Cambridge, who made the year pleasant as well as profitable. And a special word of appreciation is given to my colleagues on the faculty and administrative staff at Calvin Seminary for bearing willingly the extra burdens occasioned by my absence.

–J. H. K.

MAJOR ECUMENICAL CONFERENCES

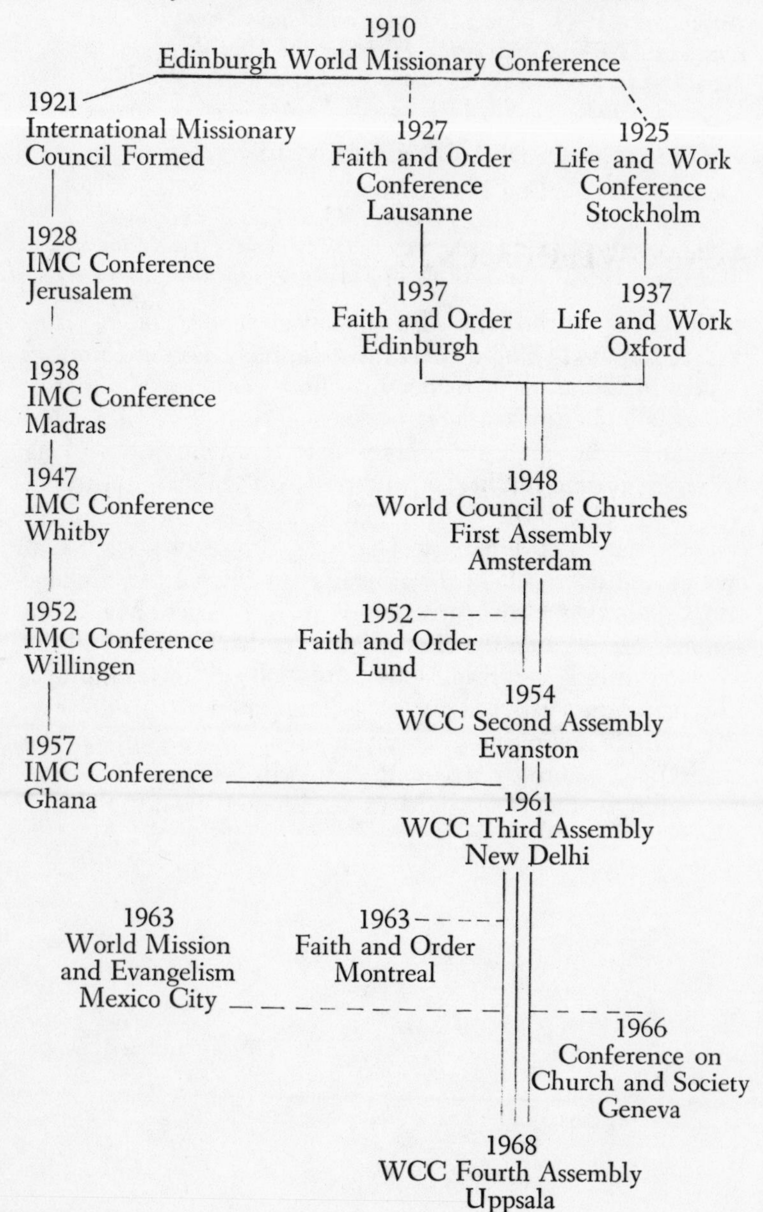

WORLD COUNCIL ASSEMBLIES

Amsterdam, 1948: *Man's Disorder and God's Design*
Evanston, 1954: *Christ – the Hope of the World*
New Delhi, 1961: *Jesus Christ – the Light of the World*
Uppsala, 1968: *Behold, I Make All Things New*

FAITH AND ORDER CONFERENCES

Lausanne, 1927: *God Wills Unity*
Edinburgh, 1937: *A Unity Deeper Than Our Division*
Lund, 1952: *The Church, Ways of Worship, Intercommunion*
Montreal, 1963: *The Process of Growing Together*

LIFE AND WORK CONFERENCES

Stockholm, 1925: *The Church's Responsibility for the Total Life of Mankind*
Oxford, 1937: *Church, Community, and State*
Geneva, 1966: *Church and Society*

MAJOR MISSION CONFERENCES

Jerusalem, 1928: *The Challenge of Secularism*
Madras, 1938: *The Christian Message in a Non-Christian World*
Whitby, 1947: *Partners in Obedience*
Willingen, 1952: *Mission in Unity*
Ghana, 1957: *Proposal to Merge with World Council*
Mexico City, 1963: *Joint Action for Mission*

CHAPTER ONE

A HOUSE DIVIDED

NEVER IN ALL THE HISTORY OF THE CHRISTIAN CHURCH has so much been said or written about the church as in the half-century of the growth of the Faith and Order Movement. Never has there been such intense attention to all conceivable aspects of the subject, never such feverish studies or earnest probings. Not even in the days of the Protestant Reformation was the church so conscious of itself. Comparisons and formulations were indeed found then, but by no means such introspection and self-analysis as today.

The momentum of such studies would indicate that the doctrine of the church is a very lively subject indeed. This is said in the face of the opinion of some that the day of doctrine is done and that systematic theology is a thing of the past. Such a sentence of doom is probably premature. In sharp contrast to this gloomy opinion is the position that "the doctrine of the church has hardly passed its pretheological phase."[1]

It is true, of course, that many elements in the contemporary

[1] George Florovsky, quoted in Colin Williams, *New Directions in Theology Today:* Vol. IV, *The Church* (1969), p. 11. Similar utterances have come from various sources, including Roman Catholics, who point to a lack of definition of the church in Roman Catholic theology prior to Vatican II. Cf. Karl Rahner, *Studies in Modern Theology* (1965), Preface.

studies of the church do not fit into the traditional categories of theology. It is also true that the agonizing, and sometimes unbalanced, self-analysis in which some have engaged has produced some very gloomy pictures of the relevance of the church and some dire predictions as to its future. But the sheer volume of studies indicates that, however its shape may be altered, there will be a doctrine of the church in the years to come.

The core of the problem has been the attempt to produce one doctrine in the place of many, whether by combination or substitution or some other means. This is the unifying theme behind the new directions and false starts, the comparisons and compromises, the reports and conclusions and the search for hidden factors. Contrary to common opinion, it is not so much an effort to *create* a new entity as to find an adequate description of an entity which, it is believed, God has already created and given. There have been many ecclesiologies devised and adhered to by many churches. But since each has practically, if not theoretically, excluded something that was really church, none was adequate for the church that is Christ's Body. It is this adequate description which has been the goal of the search. It is the halting progress toward this goal and the concern for what has happened to the various ecclesiologies in the process which is the subject of this book.

As this intensive study has gone on, there have been shifts in direction as well as waves of optimism and troughs of pessimism. Nevertheless it has been carried on with admirable steadiness and stubbornness. There is a rhythm to this exploration. Prior to the founding of the World Council of Churches (1948) there was a gradual growth in the awareness of a church behind the churches, dramatically reflected at the Oxford Life and Work Conference of 1937 in the slogan, "Let the Church be the Church!" and in the theme of the Madras Missionary Conference in 1938, "The World Mission of the Church."[2] After the founding of the World

[2] Dr. J. Mackay details these developments with admirable clarity in the *Bulletin* of the Department of Theology of the World Alliance of

Council of Churches there were three main phases in the study, corresponding roughly to the periods between the major assemblies of the council. Colin Williams describes the first of these three periods as consisting in the search for a common ecclesiology in the continuities behind our divisions and in the rediscovery of the high-church tradition. The second is marked by the realization that mission must be added as an essential mark of the church, and that the church occurs in the event of faith and obedience. In the third period, ecclesiology is moved out of the center, because the church is not an end in itself.[3]

It will be important to bear this description in mind in what follows. But these broad trends are only the product and culmination of much other study, carried on at other levels.[4] The clarity of the demarcation here given is visible only in retrospect, and is easily susceptible to oversimplification. Much of the story has been one of trial and error. Following the heartening discovery that the discussion of comparative ecclesiology need not be disrupting came the discouragement of discovering that such discussion was a dead-end street. Great excitement was then felt at the suggestion that nontheological factors, or tradition, or renewed biblical sudies might hold the key to church unity. Thus far, however, each new tack, while producing some gains, has fallen short of the promise originally claimed for it. It should be observed that such efforts, even if not currently popular, are important, since a theme once proposed and then shelved may forge to prominence again at any moment. It may also be observed that, like all sorts of changes, changes in approach to this problem are occurring at an accelerated rate in our day. No attempt will be made at this moment

---

Reformed Churches and the World Presbyterian Alliance (henceforth designated *WARC Bulletin*), Vol. VIII, No. 4 (Summer, 1968).

[3] Williams, *op. cit.,* pp. 14f.

[4] Many other scholars have set their hands to detailing this study. Examples are Albert C. Outler, "From Disputation to Dialogue," in the *Ecumenical Review* (henceforth designated *ER*), Vol. XVI, No. 1, p. 14, and Paul Minear in the editorial introduction to *Faith and Order Findings* (1963), p. 7.

to detail or evaluate the shifts in approach. Such treatment must be reserved for later chapters of a less preliminary character.

What this activity reflects is not by any means a brand-new awareness of Christian unity. Such an awareness has been present in various forms in the Christian church in every age. Even Christian groups and churches allegedly immersed in themselves may have had much more of this awareness than is usually suggested. What is new and revolutionary in the contemporary ecumenical movement is the vision of the fact that it is not the Christian individual but Christian *churches* which have to wrestle with the problems of disunity. This realization has not come easily to a Protestantism accustomed to nondenominational and superdenominational cooperation as the chosen method of acting together. And in the face of the difficulties that are presented by official relations between churches, the realization continues to have a rather precarious existence. The rediscovery and concentration upon the church is not something to be accepted with complacency and taken for granted. It is not impossible that it may be lost. The contemporary spirit of radicalism and revolution has invaded this area as well as others. There are many voices today predicting the death of the church, and many signs that they may be right. Some of the most earnest ecumenists, indeed, are welcoming this death as the necessary prelude to rising again in newness of life. In fact, not all are certain that the resultant resurrection will take place, and a few even seem to question whether it should.

On the other hand, the realization that Christian unity is preeminently the concern of the churches has deep roots. The very fact that it was hard-won lends it greater stability. The fact that the Roman Catholic Church is finally on the verge of dealing with Protestant communions as churches will undoubtedly lend new strength to it.

This rediscovery of the church, one of the great theological facts of our time, is a development that ought to have gladdened the hearts of all those for whom the church is an item of faith and an object of love. This includes those who are often designated "conservative evangelicals." Particularly those churches which had not lost themselves in rank individualism, but clung tenaciously to the creeds of the Reformation age, might have been expected to welcome this development with open arms. To a large extent this has not proved to be the case. Perhaps some of the reasons for this failure can be uncovered in the following pages, and the attempt to do so will be one of the objectives of this book.

What makes the reunification of the churches so difficult is the fact that each of them has its own doctrine of the church. Each of these respective doctrines of the churches raises high walls, designed to keep truth in and error out. The existence of such a doctrine of the church is a pervasive fact. It is not found exclusively in churches that have a high doctrinal consciousness. Churches that find their mode of existence centered in liturgy or order rather than doctrine have a doctrine of the church which, though only implicit, is no less real than one more formally stated. Churches that have an antidoctrinal loyalty also have, likewise in implicit form, a center of organization which they are reluctant to abandon and to which they invite the adherence of other churches in order that unity may result.[5]

Against such a background, no surprise need be occasioned by the continued existence of divisions after sixty years of effort. If anything, it is amazing that these churches have persisted in holding together at all. What is interesting, however, is that there has been more clarification in other doctrines than in the one that the churches most desired to clarify. Professor H. Berkhof has noted that the doctrine of the church has been peculiarly resistant to change. New biblical studies, he says, have produced many new understandings and ecclesiological expositions that do not betray their ecclesiological origins. But "this agreement suddenly finds its hard limits when it comes to the problem of the structures" of the church.[6]

---

[5] Cf. Bernard Leeming, *The Churches and the Church* (1960), p. 72.
[6] H. Berkhof, in *WARC Bulletin,* Vol. VIII, No. 4.

Nevertheless, something must have happened to these theological walls of separation between the churches. In the mergers of some churches with each other and in the growth of the World Council of Churches there has been some advance toward the unity of the church. How much advance is a matter of dispute. Some say it is not great; they assert, in fact, that it is disappointingly small. Others find it so great as to be an ominous threat. But however great or small, any progress toward unity calls for explanation. Even the mere fact that churches continue in dialogue with each other calls for comment. For the respective doctrines of the church, existing in rivalry with each other, seem to call for anathema rather than dialogue, let alone joint statements. Each seems logically to call for the unchurching of all others. It will be one of our concerns to examine the attacks made upon these walls of division in order to discover what accounts for the measure of unity that has been realized.

The fact that the walls of separation have not proved easy to deal with is due to a large number of factors. It would be impossible to present a complete list of them, but some of the more prominent ones will be briefly described here. (1) The walls of separation are buttressed by theoretical argument from real or alleged principle – and whether the principle is real or alleged makes little difference for the persistence of the argument. (2) Around the basic points of doctrine many practices have been assembled, so that the differences between one doctrine of the church and another consist not just in a few isolated ideas, but in a whole complex of activities. Ways of worship, standards for the ministry, the administration of the sacraments, and the conception of church membership are only a few of the many complexities in which the doctrine of the church is involved.[7] (3) A difficulty arises from the fact that these doctrines of

[7] "The *Report* of the Theological Commission on *The Church* observes that 'some points of difference, small in themselves, may actually be matters of major importance, because divergent positions represent diverse *total systems*. Conceptions of the Church differ not only at specific points, but give rise to rival *systems* of Christian faith and practice.' " Leeming, *op. cit.*, p. 168.

the church are so different; different in a peculiarly frustrating way. The very role played by doctrine differs radically from church to church. Churches whose doctrinal systems are very explicit find it very hard to converse with churches with a more implicit system. There is an aggravating difficulty in finding the basis on which all can converse with each other. (4) But, paradoxically, another difficulty is found in the fact that these respective doctrines of the church are sometimes not very different at all. The variances between whole families of churches, not to mention churches of the same family, are often so slight as to appear to occasion little difficulty. The real source of separation often lies not in contrasting principles, or even contrasting formulations of the same principle. Often the real cause of separation is an application or interpretation of the standards which, however politely, unchurches the other party. Because it lies behind and beneath the stated positions, this attitude defies both definition and rational argument.

(5) A further problem arises from the fact that the divisions are hardened by tradition, through which a whole complex of activities and attitudes has arisen which obscures any attempt at a fresh view. Such traditions are the more resistive to change because they are bolstered by arguments from Scripture. To their adherents living in isolation they appear very plausible and final. Their absurdity is evident only when it is seen that rival groups have substantially the same kind of stance, in which only a few details are different. (6) In the course of years, or even centuries, of living in isolation from each other, Christian churches have poured widely differing meanings into terminology used throughout the church. When at long last they come together, they discover to their delight that they sometimes agree when they think they are disagreeing. But they also discover that they often really disagree on formal statements that sound acceptable to both parties. Thus Christians discover that even they — to say nothing of ordinary mortals without their common heritage and purpose — cannot communicate meaningfully with each other without a great deal of difficulty.

(7) The high expectations that might be held regarding extensive dialogue between churches are also in need of some modification. Even in the highly structured, very official dialogues that take place within the structure of the World Council of Churches, it cannot really be said that *churches* are in dialogue with each other. Representatives, often very officially appointed, do enter into dialogue; but they find it impossible to carry back to their churches an adequate sense of the insights gained in the discussions. Often what must be communicated is an atmosphere, an intimation, or a mood. These are hard to set down in propositional terms. And this difficulty is aggravated by the lethargy, unconcern, or even suspicion of many of those who will have to accept alterations if two churches are ever really to be one. (8) A final source of difficulty concerns an old problem with a new face. The question of the source of authority in the church has long been a bone of contention, particularly between Rome on the one hand and the churches of the Reformation on the other. In the present day there would seem to be little problem in the formal identification of the sources of authority. Every party to the discussions now professes to swear by the Bible, and each is also willing to give more than a passing nod to tradition. But there is such a wide difference in the way these sources of authority are applied that one party would hardly recognize the practice of the other as authentic. And to add to all the other complications, these differences of interpretation now cut across traditional, confessional, and denominational lines.

The difficulty in arriving at a unified doctrine of the church — which is what the ecumenical movement will have to accomplish if respectable unity is to be achieved — is compounded by an additional problem of a different dimension. It has already been pointed out that each formal doctrine of the church is bound up with a host of associated practices and customs — a system, ministry and ordination, what the ministry is qualified to do and how it is done, the number, nature, and efficacy of the sacraments, and much more. A further and most significant fact is that this comprehensive doctrine of the church cannot be isolated from other doctrines adhered to by each church. The earliest clear recognition of this fact came in connection with the person and work of Jesus Christ.[8] Not only was it realized that differing ecclesiologies were rooted in differing Christologies, but there were those who argued that ecclesiology is Christology and Christology ecclesiology.[9] There is, of course, a sense in which this is an oversimplification, as has been argued by Edmund Schlink.[10] But it contains a profound truth. The church cannot be known, indeed it cannot exist, without Christ and the knowledge of Him. If therefore it should be the case (and we will argue presently that it is) that there are profound differences among the churches on the doctrine of Christ, a further and most substantial problem is inserted into the work of discovering an ecumenically tenable and applicable doctrine of the church.

But from this introductory point the problems continue to mount. What future does the church anticipate, and how does it understand its present existence? The question of eschatology cannot be avoided. Here, once again, seeming agreement quickly fades. It is quick, simple, and easy to say that we are living between the times. But what does this mean? Again, it has been recognized for some time that the much neglected doctrine of the Holy Spirit is of the most vital importance for the church. As a consequence of this recognition, the movement has undertaken extensive studies of the Holy Spirit. And yet the question how the work of the Spirit is to be recognized in the world today continues to be one of the great bones of contention in the movement. To go one step farther, one of the more recent discoveries is the awareness that the understanding of man

---

[8] Although this connection had been suggested much earlier, it came to clear recognition at the Faith and Order Conference in Lund in 1952. Cf. Minear, *op. cit.*, p. 3.

[9] This position is attributed to K. L. Schmidt. Cf. Emil Brunner, *Dogmatics:* Vol. III, *The Christian Doctrine of the Church, Faith, and the Consummation* (1962), p. 35.

[10] Edmund Schlink, *The Coming Christ and the Coming Church* (1967), p. 96.

is also related to ecclesiology, and that differences of evaluation of new motifs in this doctrine are rising to crucial importance. So the whole area of theological anthropology can be added to the list of interrelated doctrines.

Thus one might go on to add doctrine to doctrine, perhaps to no point. There is one other doctrine, however, which must be mentioned before we turn to other concerns. Underlying all of these problems is the question of the source or sources of authority on which the church bases its self-understanding; and even more crucial in our day the question of the way in which that source or those sources are interpreted and applied. This doctrine, as well as that of Christology, will be referred to again in this book, since they mark crucial points of evaluation in the ecumenical movement.

In struggling with these problems, the ecumenical movement is afflicted by the fact that it is a movement. This is both its glory and its weakness. There has been an acceptance of this fact from the beginning, and even an emphasis and insistence upon it for the benefit of those who did not understand it. It has long been recognized that the effort to express the unity of Christ's church cannot be wholly confined within traditional categories or adequately transmitted in familiar terms. The patience of participants and observers was requested on this score. It was also frequently stated, even in the early years, that participation in the movement involved a willingness on the part of the denominations to die in order to be born again into a new unity. These were brave and realistic words, but the fulfillment of this prophecy could not be predicted in detail. The progress of the movement is open-ended. The ecumenical statesmen knew where they started, but could not know exactly where they were going. The actual developments have brought surprises for some and disappointments for others. In particular it has been discovered that for a denomination to undergo a willing death for the sake of something better is more easily said than done, particularly when that better thing is still very indistinct and uncertain in its outlines.

Increasingly in recent years the movement has had to cope

with a dimension of this willingness to die which could not have been wholly anticipated. There is a growing impatience among some of its participants with the whole ecumenical procedure. Many, although not all, of those who are impatient feel little concern for unity for its own sake. The most vocal spokesmen are concerned only for witness; what happens to unity in the process is of little moment. The impatience of some reaches the point at which they are willing to forego the unity of the churches, and the efforts to achieve that unity, and operate with the unity of Christian individuals and groups. This has some of the earmarks of a curious reversion to the days of the Evangelical Alliance, prior to the emphasis on the role of the church, and prior to all the laborious concern with the comparison of old doctrines and the search for new ones. But there is a difference, a radical one. Now it is beginning to be argued that perhaps the church itself must die – not merely a denomination here or there, but the whole structure – in order to make room for some wholly new sort of presence in the world. It should be acknowledged in passing that this emphasis is not restricted to the ecumenical movement nor wholly caused by it. But the very claim of the ecumenical movement to be the shape of the church's future makes it, inescapably, the chief arena for the fighting out of this battle.

These are some of the difficulties confronted by the house divided. More attention will be paid to them later. It is now in point to remark that such a complex of difficulties might well lead to the disgusted abandonment of efforts to achieve doctrinal clarity. Certainly there must have been many weary moments for the participants in this effort. Certainly the critics of this doctrinal effort, who have never been silent since the beginning, are not becoming less vocal in these revolutionary times. And yet, through periods of optimism and pessimism, the effort has gone on to the present day. Whether it will continue until success is achieved no one can yet say. But if it does not, one of the most cherished visions of the founders of the movement will have been abandoned.

If the wrestling with the doctrinal problems should be abandoned, there would be no lack of judgments of the "I told you so" variety. There have been persistent criticisms from the outside of a lack of doctrinal interest and sensitivity in the World Council of Churches. Whatever may be the developments in the near or more distant future, these accusations are grossly out of keeping with the facts as of this date. Statements abound to the effect that there must be agreement in doctrine if there is to be unity in the church. Nor are these mere airy assertions. The effort that has gone into world and regional conferences on faith and order, into study committees, assembly themes, and articles in the *Ecumenical Review* is a most impressive refutation of the charge of doctrinal indifference. Surely the members of the long-lived committees did not persist out of a sheer love of committee work! It may be that there are justified accusations as to the way doctrine is handled, and anyone is free to disagree with the findings of a committee — as conferences and assemblies themselves have frequently done. But this is quite another matter from charging that doctrine is neglected.

Why have the participating churches taken on all of this effort and perplexity? There is nothing arbitrary about the decision at all. A necessity is laid upon them. These are not the problems of a mere wing or segment of the church — e.g. the left wing or the ecumenical segment. They are the problems of the whole church. Nor is the issue of unity a peripheral matter. It is one avenue, perhaps in our times the most inescapable one, of approach to the question of the church's existence and function. How is the church to serve Christ in this world? Although the problem has many aspects, this is its heart.

In confronting this problem, the whole church and every part of it participates in some way. If the problem of unity is really concerned with the acceptable service which is to be rendered to Christ, no organization can escape it and still be called church. Every church is participating in this search, although for some a parallel and independent course appears preferable, and for others the approach is primarily negative.

The question that keeps some churches outside of the World Council of Churches has little or nothing to do with the importance of unity or its relation to the church's witness. It is rather the question how and with whom participation in the search for unity must go on. In this book we shall examine how the World Council of Churches, and particularly the Faith and Order Movement, has dealt with the search. In the process of doing so we shall attempt to isolate and detail some of the aspects of the movement that have made it difficult for the so-called "conservative evangelical" churches to participate. Perhaps this sort of dialogue, which is welcomed by World Council spokesmen, will produce some fruit in what is a common search after the proper measure of obedience to Christ.

Implicit in the reference to a common search is an attitude that should be made explicit. The description of the activities of the World Council will be given with a large measure of sympathy and appreciation. If sharp words are sometimes used, they will at least be spoken in the assumption that they are addressed to listening ears and kindred spirits. This attitude has been confirmed by contact with the literature of the movement. While anyone may, and probably everyone will, have criticisms of the way in which the problem was attacked and the results that have come forth, one can only admire the seriousness and nobility of purpose in the persistent efforts made to solve it.

It is not our prerogative nor our intention to determine where faith exists and where it does not, or to pass judgment on the measure of someone else's obedience to Christ. It is abundantly evident, however, that there is a faith in God and in His purpose for His church underlying and undergirding the work of the World Council in its wrestling with the doctrine of the church. The evidence does not consist only, or most convincingly, in the basis and constitution of the council, however clearly it may be expressed there. The dogged persistence of the movement in seeking an elusive unity, in trying to express adequately a unity believed to have been given by God, is more convincing evidence by far. To have pursued that goal in the face of constant problems and repeated rebuffs and failures is the most eloquent testimony to the realism with which that faith is held. From all appearances that faith is very great indeed, seen in the willingness to entrust the future to God without knowing what that future will be. Conservatives may well lend their prayers and efforts to the end that it may be God indeed, and not some whim of the moment, which does the leading. But perhaps in their observation of and dialogue with the World Council they may themselves be moved to a greater readiness to let God do some leading of His own.

A few words should be added about the limitations to be set on the subject of this treatment as expressed in the subtitle, "The Doctrine of the Church in Ecumenical Perspective." The "ecumenical perspective" that is adopted will not attempt to cover all aspects of the very complex ecumenical movement. The center of concentration will be the work of the World Council of Churches, and more particularly the Faith and Order Movement. The chronological limits will be largely from the Lausanne Conference in 1927 through the Uppsala Assembly in 1968. Thus, apart from occasional references, there will be no direct reckoning with such other ecumenical forces as Roman Catholic ecumenism, church mergers, world confessional organizations, and the like.

The "doctrine of the church" also calls for delimitation. In this instance, however, the definition tends to broaden, not narrow the concept. It is not a closely defined idea of the church, but the whole complex of doctrines and activities and institutions by which churches define themselves that must be taken into account. Thus attention will be given to the notes and marks of the church, but also to its ministry, membership, and sacraments, its worship, order, and activities, and the like.

Within those limitations the subject will be approached from various angles. The overall objective will be to determine whether anything has happened to the respective ecclesiologies during the past forty years; if so, what it is and how successful it has been in achieving ecumenical objectives. The intention is to evaluate this process from the standpoint of a communion oriented to and loyal to the Reformed Confessions of the Reformation age. The views expressed are not those of that communion *per se,* but of the author as one member of it.

Chapter Two

A WAR OF MOVEMENT

The ecumenical statesmen who have made the Faith and Order Movement the object of their attention have realized that if the church is to be one, there will have to be a doctrine of the church suitable for that one church. They have also realized that the existence of many ecclesiologies, each adhered to by one or more denominations, constitutes a barrier to the formation and acceptance of that one doctrine of the church. Against that defensive line of church divisions they have waged a war of movement.

This war of movement has involved some false starts and some trial and error. Its results have not always been what they were expected to be. But it has not been without results. While the ecclesiology of the unified church is not yet clear in its details, forty years of effort have produced some growth in clarity as to the shape it must take and the road that must be followed to achieve it.

We shall examine five selected aspects of that war of movement. These will not be taken up in chronological order, since that would be difficult to establish in any case and might hamper, rather than help, the discussion. Some flexibility must also be allowed for combining the discussion of various approaches to the problem where such combination appears to aid the treatment.

It is important to remember in the discussion that will follow that we are dealing only with the theoretical side of church unity. The basis for this discussion is composed of study documents, decisions of conferences and assemblies, and theories advanced by various scholars in articles and books. These theoretical treatments of the problem of unity are addressed to individuals and churches, primarily the latter, in order that they may become one.

The real test of Christian unity comes in the question what the churches do with this advice. The principle on which the World Council and the Faith and Order Movement have operated is that action toward unity must be taken by the churches themselves. The theories, plans, and advice are effective only to the extent that they are accepted and implemented by the churches. Although this stance has occasioned some impatience within the movement, it remains the official position to the present.

This situation has some consequences for the utterances of the movement, contributing at times to vague formulation and an air of detachment. A more concrete consequence, however, lies in the reluctance of denominations to act upon the advice given. What seems clear in the warmth and light of a conference often does not appear quite so obvious when considered by a denomination. Perhaps even the delegate to the conference sounds somewhat different when he has exchanged his ecumenical hat for his denominational hat. As one study rather caustically suggests:

> Clergymen tend to talk one way when they are in denominational circles and another way when they are in ecumenical circles. Within the sphere of the denominational fellowship a minister feels strongly the compulsion to conform to the expected standards of that group, but in an ecumenical gathering there are pressures to be more responsive to other Christian bodies.[1]

---

[1] Nils Ehrenstrom and Walter Muelder (eds.), *Institutionalism and Church Unity* (1963), p. 363.

Be that as it may, we must remember that we are dealing mainly with the utterances of men while they were talking out of the ecumenical side of the mouth. To draw the conclusion that this is, finally stated, what "the church" is saying and thinking would be a considerable oversimplification.

Doctrine Divides, but Service Unites

One of the most obvious attacks on the problem of divisions is the contention that doctrine divides, but service unites. This statement is said to date from 1922,[2] and it gained official prominence at the Stockholm Conference of the Life and Work Movement. The statement as it stands is by no means to be attributed to the Faith and Order Movement. Quite to the contrary, it was an earlier version of this idea that Faith and Order originally set out to counteract. The counteraction did not take place by turning the charge around, as if to say that it is service that divides and doctrine that unites. Faith and Order would not even contend that service and doctrine tend equally to unite. But what Faith and Order stubbornly avers is that if unity is to be achieved, it will have to involve and include agreement in doctrine. And repeatedly it has been reasserted, contrary to the charges of some critics, that convictions must be honored, that repentance from divisions is not to be pretended, and that we may not repudiate separations we believe to have been carried out in obedience to the will of God.

This would seem to indicate an irreducible polarity between those who advocate and those who repudiate doctrinal agreement as the road to unity. Such a polarity does exist, and it has persisted in the movement to the present day. It may be argued that this is one of the chief internal stresses in the World Council today. Something of its current importance will be discussed in Chapter V.

But there is a sense in which this has been adopted as

---

[2] "When in 1922 at Hälsingborg, Dr. Hermann Kapler pronounced his now famous aphorism, 'Doctrine divides, but service unites,' it seemed almost self-evidently true, especially in its point about doctrine." Albert C. Outler, "From Disputation to Dialogue," *ER*, Vol. XVI, No. 1.

one of the avenues to the resolution of the doctrinal dilemma. In order to deal with it we shall have to touch briefly on such related subjects as activism, dynamism, and the mission of the church. The strategy of Faith and Order has been to avoid a sharp alternative and seek to incorporate service together with doctrine as the way to unity, by means of appropriate modifications to both concepts.

Since the beginning of its existence, the Faith and Order Movement has recognized that there is a sense in which service does unite. Already at Lausanne in 1927 it was said:

> ... pending the solution of the questions of faith and order in which agreements have not yet been reached, it is possible for us, not simply as individuals but as Churches, to unite in the activities of brotherly service which Christ has committed to His disciples.[3]

The Third World Conference, at Lund in 1952, added a striking new note to the above. There it was agreed that the churches should act together in all matters except those in which deep conviction forbade them to do so. Lund took its cue from the Epistle of James in describing the interrelatedness of doctrine and service, when it said, "A faith in the one Church of Christ which is not implemented by acts of obedience, is dead."[4] This is a note that was picked up by the Second World Council Assembly at Evanston, 1954, when it established, as the first among eight steps to unity, that the churches should act together except where this is impossible.[5] Nebulous and minor as this may appear to be, it represents the ecumenical movement at its most attractive and persuasive. Joint action is taken off the defensive, and the onus of proof rests on those who would say that a given act of cooperation is contrary to the will of God. For the World Council of Churches this conclusion marked, at least in principle, a great advance over the suspicion and rivalry that had marred the relations of churches in the past. And

---

[3] Lukas Vischer (ed.), *A Documentary History of the Faith and Order Movement* (1963), p. 36.

[4] Ehrenstrom and Muelder, *op. cit.*, p. 24.

[5] W. A. Visser 't Hooft (ed.), *The Evanston Report* (1955), p. 90.

it was evidence that Faith and Order and Life and Work were able to live together in one house, as they had agreed to do when the World Council was formed. It was a conclusion quite in keeping with the World Council's own principle of comprehending and absorbing whatever does not of itself resist absorption. The council serves a useful role here, enabling the churches to see the matter in its wholeness, instead of confronting charge with countercharge. It remains in part to be seen what the churches will do about implementing this conclusion. But they were probably able at least to recognize it more quickly together than they would have been separately.

This, however, is little more than an agreement to live together while the problem is being worked out. It does not, as such, make any real advance toward eliminating the tension between doctrine and service. But the theologians and committees have been hard at work to make such advance, and some substantial results have been achieved. The coexistence of doctrine and service has come to be interpreted not as an armistice between two enemies, but as the emergence of an essential unity that had long remained undetected. A new emphasis appeared early in the movement and accelerated in tempo as the years went by. It was the insistence that the proper means for identifying the church are dynamic, rather than static categories. The church is defined by what it does. As Colin Williams admirably summarizes the development:

> The studies began with the traditional categories, but gradually moved across to the dynamic categories of history, with attention finally focussing on the role of the church as a historical institution within God's total historical purpose. The "objectifying" categories that describe in relatively static form the "nature" of the church were seen to be inadequate. The question became that of the role of the church in the actual situation where we are confronted by God's purpose in history.[6]

---

[6] Colin Williams, *New Directions in Theology Today:* Vol. IV, *The Church,* p. 20.

Something of this development was adumbrated in the very first issue of the *Ecumenical Review,* when Nicholas Berdyaev wrote:

> The Church has hitherto been regarded as, first and foremost, a social institution, much too similar to all other social institutions. Statics prevailed over dynamics. But according to a more profound definition the Church is the mystical body of Christ and is essentially spiritual. That by no means implies that the Church should be invisible, but that it will be visible in a different way.[7]

While, slightly later, but even more directly to the point, D. T. Niles argued that the church is not adequately defined when it is defined purely doctrinally. The process of becoming in history involves nondoctrinal considerations.[8]

The first General Secretary of the World Council has summed up some of the broad trends in the progression of thought. He suggests that the Faith and Order Movement was from the beginning concerned with the centrality of Christ, but was initially too narrow in its vision of what this meant for service in the world. Life and Work, on the other hand, was concerned to express the universality of Christ's claims, while sometimes doing scant justice to the doctrinal positions that underlie the church's life in the world. The coming together of these two movements in the formation of the World Council of Churches was more than a mere formal union. The two emphases were increasingly brought together, to the improvement of each. And the inclusion of the emphasis of the International Missionary Council was only a matter of time.

> Thus "Life and Work" and "Faith and Order" had by 1937 both moved toward a deeper and wider conception of Christian universalism. It was more generally understood that the ecumenical movement would have to be definitely Christocentric, that it would have to be a movement of rediscovery and renewal of the Church, but not of the Church as an aim in itself,

---

[7] Nicholas Berdyaev, "The Union of Christendom in the Strife Between East and West," *ER,* Vol. I, No. 1, p. 21.

[8] D. T. Niles, "Our Search for Unity," *ER,* Vol. III, No. 4, p. 358.

> rather of the Church as the chosen instrument for the world-embracing saving work of Christ.[9]

The most dramatic expression of this emphasis on a dynamic definition of the church is the emphasis on the importance of the mission of the church. Missionary leaders within the World Council have long insisted that one may not just ask what the church is, but must ask what the church is for,[10] and have made mission the final criterion of the ecumenical church.[11] The Third World Council Assembly at New Delhi in 1961 may be taken as the major milestone with respect to this emphasis. Here the International Missionary Council was merged with the World Council. Bishop Neill sees this as a truly noteworthy event, in which the churches for the first time identified themselves with and took responsibility for mission.[12] But the importance of mission at New Delhi went beyond this. The New Delhi message concentrates on unity in Christ. But the expressions of that unity are centered in witness and service; i.e. not in doctrine, polity, and liturgy, the traditional three criteria of the church. Hence a fourth aspect of the church, which has gradually been rising to prominence, has come into the position of chief importance.[13]

This does not necessarily mean that other doctrines have been effectively put out of the picture, nor that all problems have been solved or all arguments ended. For one thing, the doctrine that the church is mission, while receiving great emphasis today, does not have the field all to itself. It must coexist with other doctrines, affecting them and being affected by them. The traditional doctrines are not represented

---

[9] W. A. Visser 't Hooft, *No Other Name* (1963). Although the author's concern is to document the rise of Christian universalism, his treatment of the subject lends itself admirably to the understanding of the merging of doctrinal and service emphases.

[10] Stephen C. Neill, *The Church and Christian Union* (1968), p. 76.

[11] John A. Mackay, *Ecumenics, the Science of the Church Universal* (1964), pp. 32ff.

[12] Neill, *op. cit.*, p. 108.

[13] W. A. Visser 't Hooft (ed.), *The New Delhi Report: Proceedings of the Third Assembly of the World Council of Churches* (1962), pp. 320ff.

as thoroughly obsolete, but rather as standing in need of reconsideration and refurbishing in dynamic and mission-oriented categories. It is suggested, for instance, that the sacraments might well be considered in terms of the mission emphasis.[14] Furthermore, the full effects of this new emphasis are not seen and accepted all at once. It was pointed out, for instance, that Vatican II originally had one schema for the church and another for mission, as if the two could be separated from each other.[15] In addition, it is probably still true today, as it was said to be some years ago, that there are those who resist this new emphasis in favor of a more traditional conception of the essence of the church.[16]

It may be objected that, having begun to discuss the relationship of doctrine and service, we have shifted the ground to doctrine and mission. But in view of the redefinition of mission that has been taking place in modern theology, this objection must disappear. At the least, mission is said to consist in *diakonia* as well as *kerygma* and *koinonia*.[17] At the extreme, Christian mission becomes something as yet ill defined, but something in which recognizable missionaries and a gospel that negates other religions as essentially false or fatally inadequate are considered to be things of the past. It is this consideration, in fact, which lends a further dimension to the statement that all of the problems have not yet been solved. Far more than the question whether it is proper to say that the church *is* mission, this question of the new shape of mission is likely to provoke heated discussion in the council for some time to come.

What, then, may be said to have happened to the contention that doctrine divides, but service unites? It has passed beyond the stage of mere agreement that service and doctrine can live with each other, biding their time until the victory is won by one or the other. The wheels of dis-

---

[14] Neill, *op. cit.*, pp. 190ff., and Mackay, *op. cit.*, *passim.*

[15] Neill,. *op. cit.*, p. 76.

[16] Pierre Maury, "Evangelism – The Mission of the Church to Those Outside Her Life," *ER*, Vol. VII, No. 1, p. 31.

[17] T. O. Wedel, "Evangelism's Threefold Witness: Kerygma, Koinonia, Diakonia," *ER*, Vol. IX, No. 3, p. 228.

cussion have turned to the point where it is fair to say that service *is* doctrine; at least in the sense of saying that what the church does is what defines it. What remains to be seen is whether this conception itself serves to unite or to divide.

It is not too difficult to accept this new emphasis as making a real contribution to insight into the nature of the church. The churches which have been coming to realize that they were too isolated from each other have now begun to realize that in their totality they have been too completely concerned with themselves. This is a healthful acknowledgment for any church, whether in or outside the World Council.

The problems lie elsewhere: probably not so much in the emphasis on mission as over against other criteria of the church. This may be no more than a swing of the pendulum that will correct itself in time. But there are more serious problems involved in the relationship of mission to gospel and of gospel to Scripture. It is quite proper to speak of the church as being defined by its obedience to God. But whether this is finally valid or invalid depends on the correctness with which the nature of the obedience is identified. The new emphasis on mission relies in large part on a new, dynamic, historicized view of Scripture. This, again, may be profitable. Only it must be borne in mind at all times that the concept of mission depends on the testimony of Scripture. It would be disastrous to reverse the relationship and force the Scriptures to be conformed to a preconceived notion of mission.

Again, it is to be observed that the emphasis on what the church is doing in the world is going hand in hand with the waning of emphasis on the cultic life and doctrinal heritage of the church. Which of these developments is cause and which is effect is hard to say. Taken in itself, this, as we have suggested above, need not be serious. Given the proper conditions, the cultic and doctrinal life of the church may undergo a revival and enter into a new harmony with a mission that has likewise been brought into subjection to Christ. But those proper conditions certainly must include an obedience to the revealed word of Christ. If the new presence of the church in the world is unrecognizable in terms of the gospel – a problem to which we shall return in Chapter V – the result will be irreparable loss.

Evangelicals have been much agitated over the redefinition of evangelism and the role of the church in the world in terms of changing social structures. The Geneva Conference on Church and Society in 1966 marked a peak of that agitation. Perhaps the conference was, as has been claimed, misunderstood. Perhaps also the opposition to social and political pronouncements is overdrawn at times. But if there is a likelihood, or even a serious possibility, that the new shape of the church is to be a mission that has lost the normativity of the Bible and abandoned the angularities of the gospel of Jesus Christ, then the concern of "conservative evangelicals" is not only understandable, but necessary; and it ought to be shared by many communions within the World Council itself.

That there are real problems here for the Christian church is underscored by the nagging doubt whether the cause of mission can truly be said to be flourishing in our day. If it is true, as it certainly seems to be, that the missionary force in council-oriented churches is shrinking, this is a cause for concern – even for those unaligned churches whose mission forces are expanding. What good is a marvelous new insight into the centrality of mission if there are fewer and fewer people ready to make use of it? The refuge taken from this accusation is that the mission is no longer being carried on only by professional missionaries, but is shared by a wider group. This is undoubtedly proper, although it might be argued that the change should be reflected, not in a decrease of professional missionaries but in an increase of nonprofessionals. But it is thin comfort against the background of the complaints of a loss of *élan* on the part of the average church member. If he has not been adequate to his task of witness in an era in which the world and the message were clearly identified, how is he going to become adequate now that things have grown so much more complicated and indistinct?

We would not wish to deny that "conservative evangelicals" have profited from the missionary insights of the missionaries, theologians, sociologists, and others associated with the World Council. In that sense, they need the World Council. But – what is equally ill recognized – the World Council and its member churches need the "conservative evangelicals," precisely because of their unreadiness to forsake the fundamentals of the Christian faith.

In sum, then, this particular attack on the problem of divisions has produced some real progress and insight into the nature of the church. And yet it would be wrong to judge it an unqualified success, since it has also raised problems to which the answers cannot yet be clearly seen.

The Distinction Between Essential and Nonessential Doctrines

A second wave of attack upon divisions is the distinction between essential and nonessential doctrines. The whole range of Christian doctrine, not ecclesiology alone, can be considered here. The question is not merely what ought to be the basic outlines of a doctrine of the church, but what measure of agreement in doctrine as a whole is necessary for a united church?

The distinction between essentials and nonessentials is a very old one. It is the prominence and the context of this distinction that is new. In relatively recent times, something of this sort lay just beneath the surface of the Evangelical Alliance; the idea that the things that separated Christians from each other were nonessential and could safely be ignored. This contention, however, has now entered upon a new era of seriousness and difficulty. One difference is that it is less an uncritical assumption and more a formally recognized principle than before. Another difference is that the Evangelical Alliance found it much simpler to specify what the essentials were than does the modern ecumenical movement. But the heart of the new seriousness, as well as of the new difficulty, lies in the fact that now it is the churches, not individuals, who are in conversation with each other. What will the churches do with their formulations?

This is exactly the point where the question becomes difficult. It would be hard to find anyone in the Christian world who would deny in theory that there is a difference between essential and nonessential doctrines. It is when one begins to specify what is essential, or worse still, what is nonessential, that difficulties arise. Unfortunately, that is also the earliest point at which the agreed distinction begins to mean anything.

Even if the results should finally be judged to be unsatisfactory, it is to the credit of Faith and Order and of the World Council that they attempt such a definition. Contacts established through the agency of the council have given churches the chance to observe and learn from each other. They have been able to assess their own doctrinal heritage with a measure of objectivity which any denomination by itself would have found impossible to achieve. If this were all that could be said for the council's struggles with essentials and nonessentials, they would be worth at least something. But there is more that can be said for the effort.

It would be fruitless to look for results on the most obvious level. This kind of result would consist in a formal statement by a given denomination that certain specified doctrines, once considered indispensable, were now judged nonessential. Or, in another direction, such an obvious result might consist in a denomination with an antidogmatic bias finally admitting that some statement of doctrine is necessary to a united church after all. Such admissions, if they have been made at all, have not been made loudly enough to be heard.

Two distinctions must be borne in mind. The first is between what the council or the Faith and Order Movement say and what the member denominations say. The council has said both: that certain doctrines, or subdoctrines, are not essential; and that some doctrinal agreement, and the statement of it, is essential. But whether these positions have won agreement on the part of member denominations has not been so clearly stated. Here the second distinction comes into play. It is altogether possible at any time, and altogether likely in our day, that what a denomination tacitly agrees to and what it states formally are not exactly equal to each other. The mere fact that the denominations have reduced or ended polemics is a sign that some doctrines are no longer considered essential, even though this is not formally stated.[18] Such a reduction in polemics has taken place, and it can hardly be questioned that the existence and activities of the World Council have contributed to this result.

In the direct approach of the World Council to the problems of essentials and nonessentials, several real gains can be cited. None has as yet come to its full fruition; but so far as they have developed, they show some progress. First, a model has been provided for determining which items of doctrine are fixed and which are flexible. In one study it is suggested that a distinction is to be made between order and organization. Theological dignity is possessed by the basic structure of the church, consisting of three dominical institutions: gospel, sacraments, and ministry. These are acknowledged by all churches, but expressed in varied and changing forms.[19] Another example of the same approach came early in the movement, when the Edinburgh Conference (1937) addressed itself to determining what kind of agreement was necessary for what kind of union. Several important things were said about the sacraments. It seems that the conference considered the differences in conception of the manner of Christ's presence in the Lord's Supper to be nonessential.[20] But a reconciliation as to the number of the sacraments or their very presence in the church (a ques-

[18] We recognize that certain denominations have made formal statements changing the framework of their adherence to their confessions. This is in a sense a "formal statement." This process, far advanced in some denominations before the birth of the World Council, does not, however, specify which doctrines are nonessential. All are equally affected.

[19] Ehrenstrom and Muelder, *op. cit.*, pp. 29f.

[20] Vischer, *op. cit.*, p. 57.

tion on which Eastern Orthodoxy would stand at one pole and the Society of Friends at the other) is necessary for full corporate union.[21] On the subject of the ministry, the conference judged that lack of likeness in orders was no obstacle to cooperative action. But for full intercommunion and corporate union it will be necessary to reconcile the differences between churches that hold to the following four views: (1) that a ministry in the threefold form of bishops, priests, and deacons was instituted in the church by Christ; (2) that the historic episcopate is essential for corporate union; (3) that a ministry was instituted by Christ in which bishops as distinct from presbyters are not essential; (4) that no specially ordained ministry whatsoever is required by the conception of the church.[22] Such statements require little courage when they are made by one denomination viewing another from a distance. But they call for real conviction when the objective is to bring and hold together many denominations, some of whom will say that too much has been specified, and others too little.[23]

This accomplishment must not be exaggerated. This is as yet no clear blueprint for union. One may argue that the line between essential and nonessential is drawn at the wrong place. Or he may point out that for actual union somebody is going to have to surrender something, and it remains to be seen whether that willingness will grow to workable proportions. Both of these arguments, in fact, combine with each other to stiffen resistance to mergers on this basis. But what is gained is the opportunity for churches to stand aside from themselves and reassess the relative importance of items in their own doctrinal heritage.[24] Slight though this may be,

---

21 *Ibid.*, p. 66.

22 *Ibid.*

23 Such doctrinal utterances are all the more remarkable if one agrees that the two movements that most clearly prepared the way for the ecumenical movement were the Evangelical Alliance and the Enlightenment, both of them antidogmatic. Cf. the review by Roland Bainton of Rouse and Neill, *A History of the Ecumenical Movement,* in *ER,* Vol. VI, No. 4, p. 424.

24 There is nothing, in fact, to prevent nonmember churches from mak-

it is a gain, and it is reinforced by the sheer exercise of talking and working together, which in the modern ecumenical movement is carried on as at no other time in modern history.

The second promising development is theologically much more profound. It consists in the serious consideration of the fact that all ecclesiologies find their center in Christ. This seems so obvious that it is hard to think of it as a discovery. But the fact is that the churches needed to have their attention drawn to what was implicit in the theology of each. This discovery is attributed to the Lund Conference.[25] This conference said:

> In our work we have been led to the conviction that it is of decisive importance for the advance of ecumenical work that the doctrine of the Church be treated in close relation both to the doctrine of Christ and the doctrine of the Holy Spirit. We believe that this must occupy a primary place in the future work of this movement, and we so recommend to the Faith and Order Commission.[26]

This recommendation was carried out, and its fruit is reflected in part in a statement adopted by the Third Assembly of the World Council at New Delhi in 1961:

> We acknowledge the fact that we recognize the same Christ through a variety of corporate traditions, of long or short history, and more or less clearly defined, but within each of them certain crucial elements are always preserved.[27]

Certain dangers attend this emphasis, and these have not escaped the attention of ecumenical scholars. T. F. Torrance

---

ing the same kind of assessment in the light of the published findings of the World Council.

[25] Paul Minear (ed.), *Faith and Order Findings* (1963), p. 3.

[26] Vischer, *op. cit.*, p. 92.

[27] *New Delhi Report*, p. 126. H. P. Van Dusen makes a much more sweeping judgment when he says, "If there is a single finding which stands forth with indisputable clarity from more than two decades of ecumenical examination and debate regarding the credal basis of our existing denominations, it is that, on the basic issues of Christian belief (excepting only the doctrine of the Church), there are no determinative differences." Van Dusen, "The Significance of Conciliar Ecumenicity," *ER*, Vol. XII, No. 3, p. 317.

has pointed out that Christ is the church, for the church is church only in Him. But this is not to be reversed. ". . . nothing could turn the whole Gospel upside down so quickly or so radically as to assert that the Church is Christ."[28] And Joseph Sittler has noted that when the connection between Christ and the church has been recognized, the implications still have to be drawn and applied.

> The profound studies of Christ and the Church, while they show us clearly where our life and our centre is, do not automatically furnish forth a common faith, or draw us toward a faithful ordering of the life of the church in history.[29]

How shall we assess this wrestling with the concept of essential versus nonessential? A word of caution must first be sounded. It must not be supposed that the solution to the ecumenical problem has now been found. No matter how sound the principle, the gap between theory and implementation has yet to be bridged. But that the search for the solution should be carried out in this direction is beyond dispute. Not the World Council of Churches alone, but any ecumenical organization, any fellowship of churches, any union negotiations can proceed only on the basis of a willingness of churches to distinguish between those truths which they must retain at all costs and those of which this is not true.

Again, it must be pointed out that this emphasis is evidence that the World Council of Churches is not uninterested in doctrine. A denomination may differ radically, even violently, with the council's judgment as to the essentiality of a particular doctrine. But the accusation of lack of interest in doctrine is not at present valid.

The temporal qualification is interjected into the above statement because there is a possibility that the whole doctrinal emphasis may be bypassed by a dynamistic drive that pays scant attention to any kind of doctrinal formu-

28 T. F. Torrance, "What Is the Church?" *ER,* Vol. XI, No. 1, p. 9.
29 Joseph Sittler, "Called to Unity," *ER,* Vol. XIV, No. 2, p. 184.

lation. This is the trend. The question is where and when it will be arrested, if at all.

It is also necessary to ask in all seriousness whether the World Council has not been overly optimistic about the measure of agreement. When New Delhi noted that "we all recognize the same Christ," was this a papering over of deep differences? This question has somewhat more substance than the mere suspicion of an outside observer. It was at this same assembly that the council basis was expanded. This exercise called forth new versions of old objections, both to the revision and to the basis itself. When there is persistent opposition to the statement that the World Council of Churches is a fellowship of churches that confess the Lord Jesus Christ as God and Saviour, is it really the same Christ who is recognized? Or do the various descriptions of differences among the churches consistently ignore the damaging one between a humanistic and a supernaturalistic approach, a difference, to be sure, which is no respecter of denominational lines? We reiterate that the movement has done well to focus on Christ; this is the ecumenical question *par excellence*. But one must not be too hasty in concluding that the question, "What think ye of the Christ?" has been thoroughly and satisfactorily settled among the churches of the council.

Useful as the distinction between essentials and nonessentials is, one must not ask too much from it. The profoundly important statement that what unites us is more important than what divides may tend to become so axiomatic as to be meaningless. What unites, it appears, is more important simply because it unites. Furthermore, there is one sense in which the distinction is difficult, if not impossible to apply, and another sense in which it is dangerous. The difficulty consists in the fact that nearly every doctrine of nearly every church is an integral part of a well-knit whole. The danger to be noted is that one becomes so grandly objective about his traditional doctrinal position that he is finally uncommitted to anything at all. The unitive tendency is and must always be toward less and less insistence upon essentials. A peculiar measure of grace is required for an organization committed to the promotion of unity to know how much of uncommittedness to doctrine is too much. In this respect, it is regrettable that the conservative Protestant voice is not heard more loudly and clearly in the council than it is; though this, to be sure, is not the council's fault. This is the more regrettable because there is a tendency to hold that *all* the points emphasized by traditional theology are unimportant, and that the real issues are something other than those.

One may ask also whether the council is remembering with sufficient consistency the difference between its present role and its objective. The measure of agreement in doctrine that is required for a council on the road to unity is presumably less than that which is required for a church merger, or for intercommunion, or even for public utterances in the name of the council. Council spokesmen rightly ask outside critics to bear in mind the unique character of the council when evaluating its basis. The question is whether the council itself bears this in mind. Or does it suppose that what is adequate as a basis for discussion is also adequate as a basis for witness to a world of unbelief?

It is proper to emphasize the fact that the Bible presents unity in faith rather than unity in doctrine. It is wholesome to distinguish between truths and their formulation. One may very well say with New Delhi:

> In our consideration of next steps towards an agreed doctrinal basis for the unity we seek, two useful distinctions may be made — that the intellectual formulations of faith are not to be identified with faith itself, and that *koinonia* in Christ is more nearly the precondition of "sound doctrine" than vice versa.[30]

But when this has been said, and the profound truth it reflects has been recognized, it still remains necessary to know and to say what that faith is in which the New Testament would have us be one, and which the formulations seek to describe. It is still necessary to say who the Christ is in whom we have *koinonia*. If the ecumenical question

[30] Vischer, *op. cit.*, p. 155.

is, at its very center, the question of Christ, that question remains when every formulation has been put to the test. And it remains to penetrate the *koinonia,* making it more sweet or less sweet, depending on the measure of accord reached on this question; making it, in fact, possible or impossible, depending on the agreement or disagreement on the essentials of the answer.

Creeds and Confessions

The subject of confessions arises naturally out of the consideration of essential and nonessential doctrines. The confessions of the churches may loom up as assembly-points for all sorts of nonessential doctrines, which constitute an obstacle to unity as long as they claim adherence. They may also appear, however, as guides to those doctrines which are indeed essential and not to be neglected at any cost.

Many of the churches involved in the ecumenical movement attach a particular importance to the question of creeds and confessions. Not all, to be sure, share that evaluation. Some churches repudiate all creeds, making such a repudiation practically a credo in itself. Others center their adherence to tradition in liturgy rather than confessional standards. Yet for most, if not all, the real question is not whether some confession exists, but what form it takes. Vilmos Vajta was probably correct when he wrote,

> Every church is characterized by a loyalty to its "confession," namely to a confession which forms its appearance to the world, a confession which is its unifying principle, a confession which may be written, orally preserved, or ritually mediated. For every church confesses Christ in its preaching and in the way it administers the sacraments, and by the way in which it discharges its holy call to be the servant of Christ in the world. But . . . this "confession" . . . becomes apparent with special clarity in that instance in which a church engages in a unity conversation with other churches. Then that point emerges on which she will not compromise.[31]

Our principal concentration will be on the formal, written

---

[31] Vilmos Vajta, "Confessional Loyalty and Ecumenicity," *ER,* Vol. XV, No. 1, pp. 29f.

confession. There are many different attitudes to confessions in our day, some of them reflecting denominational shifts of emphasis in the past century or less. It is instructive to consider the relationship of the World Council of Churches and the Faith and Order Movement to these varieties and shifts of attitudes.

Many of the current varieties of attitude are manifestations for which the World Council of Churches is neither to be blamed nor praised. They have taken place independently of the World Council, and in many instances prior to its formation. Long before the council came into existence there were some denominations for whom it was a basic tenet that the churches should exist without formal confessions. Among the younger churches, on the other hand, there are many that have only a borrowed confession, to which they do not lend the same measure of devotion as the churches that brought the gospel to them. To quote Vajta again:

> The peculiarity of the younger churches is that while they have a confessional origin, they do not have a confessional history of their own. Their history is one with the history of their fellow-churches in the lands in which they are situated.[32]

Other churches, however, are historically attached to one or more confessions deriving from the Reformation age or succeeding centuries. Varieties of attitudes toward such a connection are clearly reflected in the statements of comparative ecclesiology compiled in the volume, *The Nature of the Church*.[33] One such statement notes that creeds have come to be seen increasingly as testimonies of faith, rather than tests of faith.[34] Among the European Reformed churches a rather general trend toward looser contact with the creeds

---

32 *Ibid.*, p. 26, quoting a report to the East Asia Conference. This statement, however, must not be accepted without some qualification. There are "younger churches" that have shown a greater attachment to the confessions they inherited than have the churches from which they inherited them.

33 R. Newton Flew (ed.), *The Nature of the Church* (1952).

34 *Ibid.*, p. 256.

is noted.[35] The Gereformeerde Kerken in the Netherlands and the Free Church of Scotland (neither of them a member of the World Council) are singled out as examples of a firm commitment to a creedal position.[36] A particularly frank statement, reflecting, however, a position that is not rare, is the one concerning the Methodist Articles of Religion. They are

> theological formularies deriving from an earlier situation, but they do not bring out the distinctive ethos of the Methodist faith and message.[37]

These statements reflect some aspects of the situation in which the World Council operates. If the World Council experiences great difficulty in arriving at a confessional position of its own, its problems are not greater, in the opinion of some observers, than those which would be experienced by denominations if they should set about writing a creed today. To quote a representative statement:

> Whatever may have been the situation twenty or more years ago, it is no longer true that the possibilities of an articulated form of a common faith can be more readily achieved by a Church than by Churches. Now it would often be equally difficult to obtain such an articulation within as between any of the major denominations. All we can hope for is that a common listening to the Word may enable us to move forward together. Confession of faith has become more an ecumenical than a denominational possibility.[38]

However difficult it may be to imagine how or why this should be the case, the opinion is not drastically different from one expressed seventeen years earlier:

> As to credal or theological faith, it became clear that there was as much agreement among the nine denominations as within

---

[35] *Ibid.*, pp. 104, 108.
[36] *Ibid.*, p. 108.
[37] *Ibid.*, p. 326.
[38] J. D. McCaughey in *Midstream,* VI, 3; *Consultation on Church Union Negotiations, Bossey* (henceforth referred to as *Midstream*), Council on Christian Unity, Indianapolis, Ind., p. 28. This is a report of addresses and discussion at a meeting of representatives of churches currently engaged in union negotiations.

> any one of them! That is to say, the varieties of belief cut across the boundaries of these denominations in such a manner that a united church including them all would present hardly any appreciable difference in its theological aspect from that of each separate denomination.[39]

The data presented so far paint a rather gloomy picture of the status of confessions in the contemporary church and the ecumenical movement. There is another side of the picture, however, which is at least less pessimistic. It is frequently asserted that the ecumenical movement has brought about a revival and deepening of confessional consciousness on the part of the denominations. A representative statement from a recognized leader puts the matter thus:

> Experience of the Ecumenical Movement itself has taught us not to seek easy and shallow ways of reunion through a flabby grasp of doctrine and a glossing over of our differences of belief. The Ecumenical Movement, by deepening the sense of the Church, and bringing members of widely different Churches together in Christian fellowship, has driven many Christians to seek a deeper understanding of the distinctive positions of their own churches.[40]

This attitude is in keeping with the long-standing ecumenical principle that each church should bring into the ecumenical discussion its own treasures of truth.[41] This kind of comprehensiveness, in which the various confessional traditions are combined in a larger and more complete whole, has the blessing of World Council thinking. It finds a response in confessionally oriented churches who report that when they have reexamined their confessions, they have found them

---

39 Charles Clayton Morrison, "The Ecumenical Trend in American Protestantism," *ER,* Vol. III, No. 1, p. 10.

40 Yngve Brilioth, quoted in Bernard Leeming, *The Churches and the Church* (1960), p. 70. Of the many similar statements we may mention those by Lukas Vischer in *Midstream,* p. 5; and Hamilcar Alivisatos, "Orthodoxy, Protestantism, and the World Council of Churches," *ER,* Vol. VI, No. 3, p. 285.

41 The source of the idea of "each bringing in his confessional position as a treasure" is a committee solution to the problem whether Anglican students might join the Student Christian Movement. Neill, *op. cit.,* p. 342.

to be more ecumenical than they supposed.[42] There can be little question that this is a common and valid experience, in the process of which the churches have come to understand their own confessions better.

A growing confessional consciousness is reflected not only in individual denominations, but in the growth of new confessional movements on a world scale. Other, older confessional movements have received a new lease on life.[43] These are not to be contrasted with the ecumenical movement. On any adequate definition of that movement they are part of it. What effect they may have on that other part of the movement which is called the World Council, however, is an interesting question. There have been and undoubtedly still are those who consider confessional organizations a side-eddy at best, and at worst a threat to the ecumenical movement. In general, however, apart from some uneasiness,[44] the official attitude of the World Council has been to recognize that confessional organizations have a real contribution to make to ecumenicity. The attitude is frequently and consistently expressed. It is well summed up by a report of the General Secretary to the Central Committee:

> And even in the confessionalism of our day there is a double recognition of the inescapable claim which the Church Universal makes upon all of us. For in most confessional movements in our time we find that the confessional heritage is redefined in the light of the ecumenical encounter, and we find also that the attempt is made to show how this confessional approach is an avenue towards rather than away from ecumenical unity.[45]

For their part, confessional organizations and individual defenders of confessions have sought to cooperate with the

---

[42] Flew, *op. cit.*, pp. 92f.

[43] Lewis S. Mudge, "World Confessionalism and Ecumenical Strategy," *ER*, Vol. XI, No. 4, p. 379; Neill, *op. cit.*, p. 376.

[44] Visser 't Hooft in *ER*, Vol. V, No. 3, p. 279. An amusing little tug-of-war between the World Council and confessional groups is reflected in the suggestion at New Delhi that the limited opportunities of youth to meet in conference ought not to be squandered on confessional meetings, but ought to be truly ecumenical, i.e. trans-confessional. *The New Delhi Report*, p. 224.

[45] Visser 't Hooft in *ER*, Vol. V, No. 3, p. 280.

World Council and alleviate fears of counterinterests. Reporting on discussions in a confessional context, one observer writes:

> ... nowhere in the ranks of the confessional organizations is there a conscious desire to oppose the objectives or methods of the World Council. The confessional movements are not conceived as "anti-ecumenical." If they have an anti-ecumenical effect, it will be because their practical and theological implications have not been sufficiently thought out. It is the thesis of this article, on the contrary, that the development of the confessional organizations offers a means of responding to certain ecumenical realities, and of dealing with them creatively, which cannot be duplicated in any other way.[46]

Among individuals who have concerned themselves with this question, none has been more deeply involved in it than Edmund Schlink, who as a loyal Lutheran and a loyal ecumenist seeks to show how these loyalties can coexist. The Augsburg Confession, he points out, "continually calls in question the churches of this confession."[47] Thus it keeps them from passing negative judgments on other denominations on the basis of criteria they themselves cannot meet. He sums up the relationship between confessions and ecumenicity as follows:

> The road to be pursued by ecumenism lies between these two dangers. The existing confessional loyalties must not be abrogated, nor must any church be prevented from taking its own confession with a new seriousness. But the traditional confession will have to be broadened and developed, under the Word of God and in face of the witness of the brethren. New stresses must be made; new insights and enrichments must be welcomed.[48]

The World Council itself, while seeking to promote unity, has encouraged its members not to compromise their convictions. It has stated, for instance, that

> penitence for division must not be hypocritical. We cannot re-

[46] Mudge, *op. cit.,* p. 380.
[47] E. Schlink, *The Coming Christ and the Coming Church,* pp. 13f.
[48] E. Schlink, "The Church and the Churches," *ER,* Vol. I, No. 2, p. 164.

> pent of our various understandings of the church unless the Spirit shows us that they have been in error.[49]

The most unequivocal statement of such a standpoint comes not in a message to the churches, but in the attitude adopted toward proselytism. Here we find one of the clearest recognitions in all ecumenical literature of the fact that not only differences of opinion but errors and heresies are known or believed to exist in the churches.

> A church which in the light of its own confession must regard certain teachings of another member church as errors and heresies and certain of its practices as abuses cannot be compelled to withdraw or hold back its views because of the churches' common membership in the World Council, but can and indeed should continue in the future to hold and express its views in their full scope. The more frankly a church states its views in the Council or within the ecumenical framework, the less will be the need to state them in a round-about or undesirable way.[50]

One could hardly ask of the Faith and Order Movement or the World Council of Churches a more congenial attitude to confessions than they have shown to date. Granting that they are committed to the uniting of the churches – and apart from that it is senseless to speak of their role – they can hardly be expected to take a stand for one confession against all others. But where an obsession with unity might have led to a slighting of confessional conviction, this has been carefully avoided by the movement.

These data might well lead to the conclusion that all is settled and peaceful between the ecumenical and confessional emphases. The fact is, however, that there are great tensions in this area, and that the outcome of their interplay is impossible to predict. The World Council of Churches is being pulled, not two ways, but many. Not only is it confronted by many different confessions, but by many interpretations of what constitutes a confession and how it should operate, and by widely varying attitudes to the question whether confessions are tolerable or not. At one extreme

---

[49] *The Evanston Report,* p. 89.
[50] Vischer, *op. cit.,* p. 192.

is the attitude that all other churches should come over to the stance of one particular church. Although this attitude is subtly present in many churches, it received such an extreme expression by Eastern Orthodox delegates to the Second Assembly as to be almost a caricature:

> Thus when we are considering the problem of Church unity we cannot envisage it in any other way than as the complete restoration of the total faith and the total episcopal structure of the Church which is basic to the sacramental life of the Church. We would not pass judgment on those of the separated communions. However, it is our conviction that in these communions certain basic elements are lacking which constitute the reality of the fulness of the Church. We believe that the return of the communions to the Faith of the ancient, united, and indivisible Church of the Seven Ecumenical Councils, namely the pure and unchanged and common heritage of the forefathers of all divided Christians, shall alone produce the desired reunion of all separated Christians. For only the unity and the fellowship of Christians in a common Faith shall have as a necessary result their fellowship in the sacraments and their indissoluble unity in love, as members of one and the same Body of the one Church of Christ.[51]

At the opposite extreme is the attitude that the confessions are old excess baggage, that they raise the wrong issues, and that they are out of keeping with the shape of the church in the future. And in between is the attitude of a group of confessional organizations that seems to be trying to keep its feet on two continents at once:

> This question was prompted by the recognition that historic confessions of the faith result from an endeavour to explicate what it meant in specific situations to be faithful to the word of God. They have generally been the means by which the Church has confessed Christ in the face of specific challenge and attack. Such declarations may help but they may also hinder the Church in its endeavour to confess Christ in the face of the contemporary challenge. The same is largely true of the structures of the Church.[52]

This statement, let it be noted, came not from professional

[51] *The Evanston Report,* p. 94.

[52] Statement by World Confessional Bodies, *ER,* Vol. XVIII, No. 1, p. 92.

opponents of confessions, but from their professional proponents.

There are indications that it is going to be increasingly difficult to maintain the favorable attitude toward confessions that has persisted to the present moment. In the first place, the World Council is the product of its member denominations, and among them the commitment to creeds can hardly be said to be advancing. The advent of more and more 'younger churches' must strengthen the forces of those not historically committed to creeds. Among the churches which have traditionally held a creedal position, the list of those who are modifying their commitment is growing. To cite only two of many examples, one may mention the United Presbyterian Church in the U. S. A. and the Church of England.[53] Where mergers, particularly those of the trans-confessional kind, take place, a doctrinal statement may in some cases not even be considered necessary; and when it is, the measure of commitment to it is not likely to be great or very firmly buttressed by any formula of subscription. The defenders of confessions are tending to lay all of their emphasis on the witness of the confession to the world. The idea of confessions as a test of orthodoxy is waning, along with binding formulae of subscription and the idea of doctrinal discipline of church ministers. In an age when Protestants and Catholics alike are trying to find more room within their confessions the insistence that the church of the future must be confessionally oriented is not easy to maintain.

The trend of the times and the very logic of the movement are against the confessional emphasis. The trend toward activism takes its toll here. The fashion of the day is to speak of confession by doing rather than pronouncement. When attempts have been made to write a confession for today they have accented dynamism and activism. The concentration of the churches today is increasingly on

[53] In both of the cases cited, the change was merely the formal recognition of a state of affairs that had prevailed for some time. This fact only serves, however, to accentuate the dimensions of the trend.

what they believe *now,* instead of what was believed and formulated in an age past. And what is believed now appears to be more suited to dynamic than to propositional expression.

If the confessional emphasis is to be found in the united church that the World Council is seeking, eventually some confession must be found in which all of the member churches can join. Realistically considered, the progress in this direction is painfully slow, and time is running out. Any such agreement which could be formulated at the present would have to be so nebulous as to be meaningless. Thus the World Council of Churches may soon find itself in the unfamiliar and uncongenial role of a conservative force, asking that the advance into the future be a considered step and not a blind plunge. Otherwise impatience with the slow progress of confessional reconciliation and reformulation may deal the death blow to the confessional emphasis.

This outcome would be catastrophic. This judgment does not constitute an objection to some of the developments that seem to be impending. If, for instance, there should be an end to uncritical subscription to each jot and tittle and to the obsession with one formulation as over against another, the cause of truth would be helped rather than hindered. Such developments may be necessary, profitable, and overdue. The danger lies in the repudiation, not only of a formulation, but of the great Christian affirmations it formulated. The danger is not that the churches will abandon a form of words, but that they will forsake the reality behind the form. Some supporters of confessions have at times taken absurd positions. But the idea that the historic confessions of the church do not, in the main, focus attention on the very heart of the faith is also absurd. It is part of a critical attitude toward the confessions that is unfair, untrue, and dangerous in the extreme.

These comments, let it be said again, are not a complaint against the World Council of Churches or the Faith and Order Movement. They are much rather expressive of concern about contemporary trends in theology and churchmanship. There is something to be said for the greater measure of honesty today, when churches that have long since ceased to honor their historic confessions are finally admitting the fact openly. But this does not mean that what is thus honestly admitted is itself a good thing. The accent is laid strongly on the way in which the creeds bind the Christian. But in so far as they are correct reflections of the Word, accurate expressions of the Christian faith, do they not rather liberate? The accent is consistently laid on the manner in which rival creeds divide. But will not the forsaking of the creeds be even more deeply divisive of the church?

It is all very well to rejoice in the fact that many difficulties disappear when historical roots are forgotten and when we concentrate on what we believe today.[54] But rootlessness is not a healthy condition for the Christian church. Cutting the roots is an abandonment of the church's character. Contemporary as it may be, it *is* a historic institution. New as it must become, it *is* the same today as yesterday. The great creedal affirmations testify to its foundation on the Word and to its unity with Christ, dimensions that it can deny or ignore only at the cost of its life and character.

The tragedy of rootlessness is that the young may be swept away by the latest fad and be unable to regain their equilibrium when the fad has faded – which at today's pace takes about five years. Perhaps this sounds like a plea for intellectual inertia. But it is not. It is a plea for the momentum of Christian tradition. It is just this that constitutes a danger for the churches today – that they will lose the very traditions out of which the new understanding of the truth must come, if it is to come at all.

A Fresh Start

The fourth attack on the bulwarks of division may be designated a fresh start. It must be noted at the outset that this is not anything new in the sense of being unprecedented. There have been many attempts at a fresh start in the

[54] Neill, *op. cit.*, p. 350.

church's struggle for unity, and the history of the ecumenical movement is studded with them. The movement itself is consciously and deliberately forward-looking, ready to make some kind of break with the past in order to achieve a better future. The Edinburgh Missionary Conference, the Faith and Order Movement, and the organization of the World Council of Churches were all fresh starts. Bishop Neill[55] lists the three outstanding ecumenical events of our time as being the creation of the Church in South India, the final formation of the World Council of Churches, and the convening of the Second Vatican Council. What is distinctive about these is that now, as never before, the churches consider it their responsibility to bring the unity of the church to visible expression.

Those very words suggest another aspect of what might be called a new beginning. There has been a recent shift, especially in Europe, from the question how the fragments of the church can be brought together (achieving unity) to the question how the unity which only God can and does give can be brought to light (expressing unity).[56] This comports with and contributes to what may be called a new beginning within the movement. At the Faith and Order Conference at Lund in 1952, a shift was made from the study of the comparative doctrines of the various churches to other and more basic questions about the unity of the church, such as the relation of the church to Christ, the Holy Spirit, tradition, and social forces; and a new emphasis on biblical theology.

This provides a convenient occasion for treating several items under the one heading of a "fresh start." The three that will be considered are tradition, nontheological factors, and biblical studies. These may or may not seem to be closely related to each other. But in their connection with the Lund Conference they achieve a certain unity they might not otherwise have had. There was a consciousness within the

---

[55] Neill, *op. cit.*, p. 332.

[56] J. Dillenberger and C. Welch, *Protestant Christianity Interpreted Through Its Development* (1954), p. 299.

movement that something new was in the air. One of the committees arising out of this new impulse wrote, in preparation for the Montreal Conference:

> We have sought to understand the reality of the Church in a different way from that suggested in most conventional statements. This is not because we would reject these definitions out of hand, but because we believe that a fresh approach may help to put the questions of Christian unity in a new light, and thus facilitate discussions of the problems which our present disunity raises.[57]

One additional remark may be in order. All three of the devices that we will examine – the reconsideration of tradition, the recognition of nontheological factors, and the revival of biblical studies – may be grouped together as attempts at objectivity or detachment. Such an attempt at objectivity is inherent in the ecumenical movement itself. Even the most elementary comparison of systems of doctrine with those held by other groups is part of an attempt to get just a bit outside one's narrow circle for a better look, not only at others, but at oneself. But this new departure escalates the objectivity and detachment. Now the doctrinal systems are not only compared with each other, but each is held up for scrutiny to see what it contains that is universally valid and what is restricted; what is permanent and what evanescent.

For our purposes the examination of tradition can be briefly treated. It was very proper and right that this aspect of Christian doctrine should be singled out for scrutiny. It was also a mark of some growth in maturity and poise on the part of the Faith and Order Movement that it dared to do this. Such an approach would have been very difficult to visualize in the days prior to 1948. The study of this subject recognized Tradition with a capital "T" behind the various traditions in which Christianity exists. The presence of the latter was recognized as normal, and no criticism was raised against it. But it was noted that

---

[57] Minear, *op. cit.*, p. 30.

> the puzzling and scandalizing thing is that the different "traditions" have become contradictory and mutually exclusive, not least because of a quite different understanding and appreciation of the word tradition.[58]

Some of the ideas put forth in this study seemed unobjectionable enough. In keeping with the lines laid down at Lund, the focus was seen to be in Christ:

> Whatever may be the apparent divisions in the Church of Christ, the diversity of the confessional traditions, whatever the weight of history, one thing is certain; Christ is so consistent and so real a person that it is impossible to have anything to do with him without finding oneself in conversation with the other people who have also found him, and without this conversation being a form of his grace.[59]

The peaceful acceptance of the findings of this study was not extended, however, to all elements. Enthusiasm for a possible breakthrough in Christian divisions led to an exaggeration of the comprehensiveness of tradition. It was suggested that the relation of Scripture to tradition might be solved by seeing Scripture as part of tradition.[60] When the report was discussed at Montreal, the study section proposed that "we can say that we exist as Christians *sola traditione* — by tradition alone."[61] But this alternative to *sola scriptura* ran into great difficulty and did not meet with acceptance. However ready the churches may be to learn from a reconsideration of their own traditions, they are not yet ready to adopt a statement that sounds, on the surface though not more profoundly, like an attempt to outdo Rome at its own game.

The consideration of nontheological factors was somewhat more productive. It was admitted that the consideration of nontheological factors was not strictly new. The American study report to the 1937 Edinburgh Conference had already called attention to them. But this avenue of inquiry was

---

[58] *Ibid.,* p. 36.
[59] *Ibid.,* p. 63.
[60] Schlink, *The Coming Christ and the Coming Church,* p. 310.
[61] Patrick Rodger and Lukas Vischer (eds.), *The Fourth World Conference on Faith and Order* (1964), p. 24.

neglected for a while after that.[62] Some observers seemed to feel that this provided the real clue to the isolation of differences.[63] Nontheological factors affecting church unity are to be found throughout the church's life; doctrine, sacraments, ministry, ways of worship; Scripture and tradition.[64] One committee summed up its area of interest rather effectively as follows:

> Hence a serious understanding of unity and disunity must take note of variations in personal religious needs and interests, variations in economic and political interests, national differences, social mobility and social change, and differences deriving from the international development of the religious system — and all these should be seen as a complex matrix of interaction.[65]

The most pertinent observation to be made about nontheological factors is that they may be and often have been disguised as theological. What is actually a social or economic distinction is buttressed by being presented as a theological principle.[66] It appears to be suggested at one point that when nontheological factors causing division are recognized, they will be easier to overcome than theological factors. This would seem to be sound theological theory, but a bit dubious in ecclesiastical practice. One would suppose that if a particular nontheological factor were not a cherished position, no one would have taken the trouble to find theological arguments to support it.[67] A little later, however, the same article makes

---

62 Minear, *op. cit.*, p. 3.

63 "It thus appears that the great and well-known theological issues, which are so earnestly debated at top levels by those who are striving for unity among the churches, are not the only or even the main factors which have operated to create and maintain disunity. The real causes are to be sought elsewhere. This is, of course, not to say that the theological issues are unimportant and do not merit the emphasis placed upon them. It does mean, however, that even if such issues were all settled Christian unity would not be achieved, nor would we be able to maintain such unity as we could achieve on that basis." Elmer T. Clark, "Non-Theological Factors in Religious Diversity," *ER*, Vol. III, No. 4, pp. 355f.

64 Minear, *op. cit.*, p. 3.

65 *Ibid.*, p. 10.

66 This is recognized by Clark, although he tends to underestimate the weight of these theological arguments in the minds of theologians. Cf. Clark, *op. cit.*, p. 349.

67 Cf. Vischer, *op. cit.*, p. 104.

evident that these nontheological factors are thought to be amenable, not so much to elimination as to the idea that they can coexist in one church, seeing that they are not involved in profound theological principles.[68] Put this way, the objective of the discussion of nontheological factors seems more likely to be achieved.

The recognition and consideration of nontheological obstacles to unity is capable of bearing some fruit. It is recognized, for instance, that the union in South India was aided by some and hampered by some other such factors. Aid came from the fact that 95 percent of the members were ignorant of or indifferent to the theological niceties involved in the union, and had a racial solidarity that was stronger than their theological differences. But union was hampered by the threat of loss of position or privilege in the caste system or in relations to the wealthier missions.[69]

There has been some argument as to the validity of the designation "nontheological." One committee suggested that no factors, if they bear on the life of the church, are really nontheological. Daniel Jenkins reinforces this by arguing that the so-called nontheological forces are often really very theological. He suggests that they may have as great an effect on dogma as biblical criticism has had on Bible study.[70] This is a curious reversal of the argument. On the one hand it can be said that positions alleged to be theological are really nontheological. On the other hand, nontheological positions are really theological. This suggests the need for clarification of terms. When all due allowances have been made for the fact that religion interpenetrates all of life, it is salutary to remember that the technical methodology of the approach to nontheological factors is more likely to be that of sociology than that of theology. A conference held on the question whether sociology could help the church concluded on the one hand that the church had used sociology

---

68 *Ibid.*, p. 111.

69 Ehrenstrom and Muelder, *op. cit.*, pp. 222ff.

70 Daniel Jenkins, "The Ecumenical Movement and Its 'Non-Theological Factors,'" *ER*, Vol. III, No. 4, pp. 339ff.

too little. But on the other hand, sociology could study the *corpus Christianum,* but not the Body of Christ. Therefore the reality of the church stands outside the reach of sociology. Sociology could and should define the particularities of the objects represented in the church. At the same time, sociology must recognize, in a spirit of objectivity, that the church was determined by a special moment of revelation.[71]

In the spirit of that last comment, we should judge that while the consideration of nontheological factors is necessary and profitable, it cannot provide a final breakthrough in overcoming the divisions in the church.

The third device in the fresh start is biblical studies. If it is true, as we have said, that the study of tradition and of nontheological factors is not new, it is true *a fortiori* that biblical studies are not a new tool in the formation of Christian doctrine. It might be enough to argue in favor of renewed biblical studies on general principles. The studies out of which the church's traditional doctrines sprang have been carried on so long ago that the derivation of doctrine from the Bible has become obscure. But more than that is intended by the renewed attention to biblical studies. They are expected to bear new fruit precisely because of the new understanding of Scripture that modern scholarship has produced.[72] Thus it is argued that biblical criticism can render good service in showing the right interpretation of the Scriptures, if it is not denied the freedom to work and if it remembers its own true character.[73]

There is undoubtedly much to be said for the adoption of a program of biblical studies of church doctrine. Few Protestant denominations, if any, can be justly proud of their record of actual obedience to the Scriptures. Most of them might well ask themselves whether they are not as tradition-bound as the Roman Church which is (or at least was) often accused of neglecting the Bible – and bound all the more

[71] "Can Sociology Help the Church?" *ER,* Vol. III, No. 4, pp. 388ff.
[72] Cf. H. Van der Linde, "The Nature and Significance of the World Council of Churches," *ER,* Vol. III, No. 3, pp. 245f.
[73] Vischer, *op. cit.,* p. 44.

tightly because they do not recognize that this is the case.

But this turns out to be no panacea. The principal service rendered thus far has been to break down notions formerly held. This service is effectively summarized in these words:

> The enormous exegetical ferment which has been engendered by recent decades of brilliant and notion-cracking biblical studies makes it quite impossible to derive schematically neat ideas about worship from the New Testament community. Some old certainties have been made untenable, and a confusing and exciting richness of life has been exposed.[74]

Valuable as this may indeed be, it is hard to construct a blueprint for a united church from a "confusing and exciting richness of life."

Secondly, and more important, a good deal of homework has to be done before biblical studies can realize their promise. The present agitated state of criticism and hermeneutics is not designed to produce solid and acceptable new positions. Hermeneutical theories follow each other so fast that by the time a Faith and Order Conference or a World Council Assembly would have been able to assess the results of any study, the principles on which it was based would almost certainly have been called into question. In all seriousness, not a great deal can be expected in this situation, especially when that which these new studies seek to modify is itself a position or system that was ostensibly based on Scripture. In that situation it is not so much the ecclesiastical doctrine as the theory of hermeneutics which is fighting for recognition.

Like much else in the ecumenical movement this points to the need for agreement among the churches on their view of the authority and interpretation of the Scriptures. Such is the centrality of God's revelation that this question will not down. The best thing that can be said about the current situation is that the existence and importance of the problem is recognized. The following two recent utterances illustrate this. The first comes from a 1967 consultation of representa-

[74] Joseph Sittler, "The Shape of the Church's Response in Worship," *ER*, Vol. X, No. 2, p. 142. Cf. also H. Berkhof in *WARC Bulletin*, Vol. VIII, No. 4.

tives of churches currently engaged in union discussions. It is reported that

> the representatives at the consultation were unanimous in the opinion that one of the most important questions they face in negotiations — one which runs through all issues from doctrine to structure — is that of freedom and authority. . . . In the first instance, this is manifest in a questioning of biblical authority. The hermeneutical problem is important, but even deeper is the question whether the Bible can really be said to be authoritative at all, and if so what this means.[75]

The second quotation is an uncompromising declaration by the new General Secretary of the World Council of Churches in his report to the Central Committee in 1967:

> With no intention of entering here into the technical debate of the Biblical theologians, let me repeat that the ecumenical movement cannot be expected to survive without that awe-filled response in both worship and thought that has from the beginning been so richly received by the Church from the Scriptures, so much so that we have traditionally described the Bible as the Word of God.[76]

So crucial is this issue that we shall have to return to it in another context. It is sufficient here to remark that the tremendous potential of biblical studies in resolving the problems of unity and division simply cannot be realized until there is clarity on the nature and interpretation of the Bible.

And to add one more, half-humorous, consideration: even when a new scriptural approach is agreed upon, it will still not necessarily produce unified results. Somehow the systems can go through the mill and come out the same old systems. For one example: one of the most popular recent slogans is that which speaks of the church as event.[77] The church is pictured as something that is happening, something that cannot be captured in dogmatic categories. A fruitful thought, indeed, ringing true to much that is found in Scripture, coming like a breath of fresh air, and carrying great doctrinal

---

[75] *Midstream,* p. 69.

[76] Eugene Carson Blake in *ER,* Vol. XIX, No. 4, p. 449.

[77] A term contributed by Karl Barth to the First Assembly at Amsterdam, and becoming increasingly popular ever since that time.

and ecumenical implications in its train.[78] Faith and Order studies have taken up the church as event, and have quite properly pointed out that event is never without form.[79] The structured expression of Christ's activity is required, not only by man's historical and social condition, but by the definiteness of Christ's incarnation.

All of this sounds fine, but let us look once more. What does the church as event mean? For Barth, preaching is event, and the church comes to life only in this event. Therefore the church is also to be understood as event. Continuity breaks down. What happens to the institution matters little. The church has to be reborn every Sunday.[80] Brunner has much the same idea, and the no-church movement in Japan is something of an institutionalization of this noninstitution.

James M. Robinson, agreeing with Fuchs, seems to go a long step farther:

> Theologically speaking, proclamation is such a language event in which the body of Christ is constituted, assembled. The church as assembly takes place in the language event of proclamation.[81]

But how does the church as event appear through Catholic eyes? Quite like a Catholic institution, one would have to say:

> Therefore the Church is most tangibly and intensively an "event" where (through the words of consecration) Christ himself is present in his own congregation as the crucified and risen Saviour, the fount of salvation; where the Redemption makes itself felt in the congregation by becoming sacramentally visible; where the "New and Eternal Testament" which he founded on the cross is most palpably and actually present in the holy remembrance of its first institution. Therefore the celebration of the Eucharist is the most intensive event in the Church.[82]

Anyone can play at this game, though some better than others. Who could deny Billy Graham the right to say that this is his emphasis? The event of the church comes at the

---

[78] Cf.- Karl Rahner, *Studies in Modern Theology*.
[79] Minear, *op. cit.*, p. 28.
[80] Neill, *op. cit.*, p. 57.
[81] James M. Robinson, *The New Hermeneutic* (1964), p. 58.
[82] Rahner, *op. cit.*, p. 317.

moment of decision for Christ. They all play the game and everyone wins a prize. When the problem is solved by this kind of device, everyone has had an interesting time, but the problem remains.

One would have to say that, on balance, the promise held out by the fresh start motif is a tantalizing mirage, reflecting an image of unity that remains always just a bit beyond reach.

Growing Together

The final phase of the war of movement overlaps and supports all the others. It is the conviction that if the churches will meet together and speak and work together, eventually they will grow together. Something – just what is not known – will happen to the divisions in this process, and they will cease to divide. There is something naive and childlike about this belief. But to say this does not mean at all that it is without beauty or power or validity. The attitude is at the opposite pole from the cynical realism that pulls the church apart limb from limb – although this is not to say that the two attitudes never coexist in one person. There is implicit in this action a faith in God, in the working of the Holy Spirit, in the genuineness of the "given unity" in Christ which is very appealing indeed.

This attitude, however, is not left to exist entirely on the level of childlike faith. It is given a shape and a theological rationale. The Second Assembly performed something of this work when it outlined a program of action leading toward unity. In summary, the eightfold path of this program is as follows: (1) Act together except where this is impossible. (2) Listen together, in the midst of our disunity, to the Lord speaking in the Scriptures. (3) Consider frankly the influence of social and cultural differences. (4) Speak the truth in love and love those who disagree with us. (5) Learn the meaning of baptism and the Eucharist. (6) Recognize the true ministry outside of our own. (7) Bear united witness. (8) Pray for unity.[83] Not all of these eight steps fit equally

[83] *The Evanston Report,* pp. 90f.

well into the pattern of simply growing together, but several of them are definitely of that order.

In a more formal attempt at a theological rationale, it is pointed out that the *locus* of unity has been sought in the wrong place:

> Points of agreement have been sought in such things as doctrines and confessions, tradition and hierarchy, the Bible, codes of ethics, or personal experience. But instead of bringing about unity, all these points merely cause more division. . . . We require a category wide and deep enough to include all the points mentioned. It lies in the revelation of God in history, and this revelation in the historical Person, Jesus Christ, has taken form in the living community of the New Testament *Ekklesia.* This *koinonia* offers the only *locus* for our unity.[84]

This identification of the *locus* of unity will, in turn, have its effect on theology:

> . . . doctrinal agreement in the church cannot be obtained merely on an intellectual level, as if it were a consensus between different philosophical doctrines. Doctrinal agreement presupposes the existence of a *koinonia* of believers.[85]

What success has been experienced in the war against division is owing at least as much to this consideration as to any of the others mentioned. We must now seek to describe the process by which that success has come about, in as far as it lends itself to description.

An important aspect of the process of growing together is implicit at the very outset. There was a time when

> many men thought their own beliefs were so absolutely clear and self-evident that they found it hard to conceive that there could be elements of truth in positions other than their own.[86]

But now the matter is different:

> The fact of the ecumenical movement already means that Christian churches with their different historical origins and traditions

---

[84] J. C. G. Kotzé, "The Meaning of Our Unity in Christ," *ER,* Vol. VII, No. 4, p. 326.

[85] Roger Mehl, "The Ecumenical Situation," *ER,* Vol. XVI, No. 1, pp. 11f.

[86] R. Buick Knox, "Archbishop Ussher and Richard Baxter," *ER,* Vol. XII, No. 1, p. 50.

> — whether members of the World Council or not — have given up claiming to be exclusive, i.e., claiming that their own form of church is the only manifestation of the One Church of Jesus Christ. They cannot deny that other churches also represent a form of the Church of Jesus Christ, though less fully, and although they may see much to criticize in them.[87]

Once that kind of attitude is adopted and contact established, everything works toward an increase in understanding. As one commentator notes, "Participation in the ecumenical movement is likely to prove highly disturbing to preconceived ideas."[88] And this is true particularly of the negative ideas. As has been noted earlier, there are occasions when churches discover that when they seem to be saying the same thing, they mean something quite different. But it is far more frequently the case that contact brings about a larger measure of understanding. And even when the result of closer contact is shock at the unbelief of the other party, the estrangement is at least, in all likelihood, no greater than that which existed in the period of ignorance. Ignorance of another church's true teaching is seldom blissful.

There was some disillusionment early in the ecumenical movement over the fact that resolution of doctrinal disagreements did not come more easily. The greater optimism that has resulted from further experience does not spring from a solution of the doctrinal problem, but from the determination that it is not as much of a problem as it appeared to be. Ecumenical contacts have aided in this by helping churches to see themselves in comparison with others without employing a double standard. The dangers of a double standard included comparing the ideal of one's own church with the actual performance of another; and bearing false witness against another church in order to advance one's own.[89] Ecumenical contacts provide a multiple attack on this attitude. The ecumenical spirit, whether in or outside of the World Council, has been hard on the sectarian spirit, on the sectarian

---

[87] Hans Heinrich Wolf, "Towards an Ecumenical Theology," *ER,* Vol. XIII, No. 2, pp. 219f.

[88] Neill, *op. cit.,* p. 49.

[89] Vischer, *op. cit.,* p. 187.

elements in the respective doctrines of the church, and more particularly on the sectarian attitude to and interpretation of these doctrines. The doctrines may remain a wall of division, but the barbed wire has been removed.

The churches' approach to one another is assisted by a conscious and deliberate policy of comprehensiveness on the part of the movement. The distinction between essential and nonessential doctrines has contributed to a concentration on major points, rather than the peculiarities of various formulations. Coming out of their isolation, the churches have sought to see whether the peculiarities of various views – their own as well as those of others – cannot be understood as partially correct viewpoints on basic matters held in common. More formally, one of the study committees noted that its methodology repudiated disjunctions: Old Testament – New Testament; ontology – soteriology; Scripture – tradition.[90] This attitude appeared in an early Methodist statement on ecclesiology:

> It is . . . impossible to maintain that any one communion of Christian people, out of its own history and experience alone, can build up a complete doctrine of the nature of the Christian Church, or that any one period of history, even that of the first century itself, can furnish us with a complete statement.[91]

And this attitude receives support from those biblical studies which have sought to demonstrate that the New Testament simply does not provide us with a single church order, doctrinal system, or concept of the ministry.

The best illustration of the application of this approach to a particular doctrine is found in the doctrine of the ministry. At the first full conference of Faith and Order, Lausanne, 1927, a statement to this effect was formulated. Because it sums the matter up so well it is worth quoting at some length:

> In view of (1) the place which the episcopate, the councils of presbyters, and the congregation of the faithful, respectively, had in the constitution of the early Church, and (2) the fact that

[90] Minear, *op. cit.*, p. 12.
[91] Flew, *op. cit.*, p. 194.

> episcopal, presbyteral, and congregational systems of government are each today, and have been for centuries, accepted by great communions in Christendom, and (3) the fact that episcopal, presbyteral, and congregational systems are each believed by many to be essential to the good order of the Church, we therefore recognize that these several requirements must all, under conditions which require further study, have an appropriate place in the order of life of a reunited Church, and that each separate communion, recalling the abundant blessing of God vouchsafed to its ministry in the past, should gladly bring to the common life of the united Church its own spiritual treasures.[92]

Although adopted early in the history of the movement, this standpoint has remained in force. It was confirmed by the Edinburgh Conference in 1937.[93] And it is worth noting that precisely this standpoint is involved in the attempt by the Consultation on Church Union (COCU) to bring forth a church "truly catholic, truly reformed, and truly evangelical."

This approach is not without its problems. One author considers that the Lausanne and Edinburgh idea on the inclusive ministry reached an impasse not broken until the Montreal Conference in 1963. Montreal focussed attention on a total ministry of all church members, seen from the viewpoint of service rather than office.[94] More generally, however, there is a difficulty inherent in the very idea. Frederick Denison Maurice, following J. S. Mill, held that men are generally right in what they affirm and wrong in what they deny.[95] This has an ecumenical appeal about it, but it fails to meet the demands of a situation in which one affirmation is actually a denial of another. How, for instance, does the inclusive theory of the ministry meet the position of those who are convinced that episcopacy is of the *esse* of the church? And is there not a sense in which this approach violates the World Council's determination not to "prejudge

---

[92] Quoted in Ehrenstrom and Muelder, *op. cit.,* p. 32.

[93] Vischer, *op. cit.,* p. 60.

[94] Per Erik Persson, "The Two Ways – Reflections on the Problem of the Ministry," *ER,* Vol. XVII, No. 3, p. 324.

[95] Cf. *ER,* Vol. XII, No. 1, p. 116.

the ecclesiological problem"?[96] Inclusivism seems at first to comprehend all views. But it would certainly seem to imply that a church cannot be exclusivistic and subscribe to the spirit (rather than the letter) of the council's life. One author points out that victory for one of the theories about the nature of the church will not mean the attainment of unity, but "the collapse of unity before the victorious conquest of an exclusive dogmatism."[97] But is there no danger in an inclusive dogmatism?

Be that as it may, the churches have entered into dialogue and cooperation with each other. In spite of the difficulties involved in transmitting the results of such dialogue to the rank and file of the church, there can be no doubt that increased understanding and tolerance has resulted. Although not yet accepting one another as churches in the true and full sense of the word, they recognize the *vestigia ecclesiae* in each other.[98] But this situation does not remain static. The willingness to speak and work with one another without recognizing each other as churches in the true and full sense of the word gradually and imperceptibly evolves into acceptance in the true and full sense. There is a *de facto* recognition, regardless what the documents may say. Then the problem becomes that of getting the theory to catch up with the facts.

There is both logic and illogic about the recognition of *vestigia.* No church can consistently believe that the church exists in its wholeness outside of that church (denomination) itself. Therefore, the only thing it can do with the "marks of the church" outside of itself is to consider them as "vestigia." That is logical. But the illogic arises when each church has to grant to each other church the right to think the same exclusive things about itself.

---

96 From the "Toronto Statement"; cf. Vischer, *op. cit.,* p. 170.

97 Clarence T. Craig, "The Reality of the Church and Our Doctrines About the Church," *ER,* Vol. III, No. 3, p. 217.

98 Cf. the Toronto Statement in Vischer, *op. cit.,* pp. 173f. "Vestigia" is a term long in use, but since 1954 it has fallen into some disfavor and there has been a preference for "partial mutual recognition." Cf. Neill, *op. cit.,* pp. 31, 34.

Because this entire process is carried on with such a disregard of formulations and rationale, it is hard to analyze and hard to criticize. It is difficult to determine, for instance, what has happened in the progress toward recognition as churches "in the true and full sense of the word." Does this imply an increasingly favorable judgment on the other church? Or does it imply a reduction in what is meant by the "true and full sense of the word"? Probably it is both, but nobody can really say in how far it is either. Difficult as it is to analyze, however, it is equally difficult to deny that this process has brought the churches closer to unity.

What was necessary to bring this progress about was basically that the churches, while still remaining organizationally separate from each other, and perhaps even still looking askance at each other, were willing to refrain from unchurching one another. And one can only judge that this is a proper thing to do, but for one possible exception. What if the facts in the matter do really call for unchurching another communion? Is this the one possibility that is automatically excluded? If so, perhaps it would be better to stop speaking about any essential doctrines at all, or about a basis of fellowship for the churches of the council. The presence of this "possible exception" certainly cannot serve to negate all the good that has come from the conversations and cooperation between the churches. But the churches will do well to remember that such a problem does exist, for they could ignore it only at their own peril.

* * *

Perhaps the imagery of a war of movement against a wall of defense is inaccurate in one sense. The defense has been less like a wall than a defense in depth. Both the attacker and the defender have been on the move, shifting ground. The architects of union must have been frustrated at many points by the bewildering varieties of opinion found between and within the denominations, by the agreements within the disagreements and the disagreements within the agreements. In such a war of movement it is hard to say who has won, or what ground has been gained. For one of the rules of the war is that a contestant can claim to have gained ground even if he is unable to map it out. And yet, in spite of the obscurities and reservations, it would be impossible to deny that after all the effort the unity of the church is just a bit closer and its shape a little better defined than before the effort was begun.

Chapter Three

CONCENTRIC DOGMA

When one reviews what ecumenical theologians have said about the doctrine of the church it may appear at first glance as if the discussion has gone off in all directions. This impression is created by the fact that many novel and sometimes exotic ideas, not previously applied to ecclesiology, have been introduced into the discussion. And yet upon reflection this impression must be seen as erroneous. There is a definite centripetal movement in the increasing concentration on the central issues involved in the doctrine of the church. Perhaps an applicable image is that of a whirlpool, in which there is a great deal of motion, but a gradual trend toward the center.

There is as yet no certainty, however, that this trend will finally culminate in the emergence of a universally accepted doctrine of the church. Not only central agreements, but central disagreements as well are coming to light. There are some issues that stubbornly defy solution. The identity of these issues and their resistance to resolution are becoming increasingly apparent. This fact keeps the ecumenical movement under constant pressure. There is little likelihood that the churches will abandon the ecumenical effort because of these difficulties. What is more likely is that impatience with an apparent lack of progress, in the face of increasingly urgent demands upon the church's witness, will prompt an effort to turn the ecumenical movement in a radically new direction. Our reflections on this pressure and its possible consequences for the movement will be reserved for a later chapter. We shall limit the present discussion to the emergence of the issues.

The discussions of the various aspects of ecclesiology have concentrated on certain crucial areas. Our discussion will follow this lead. While little will be said, for instance, about the holiness of the church, much more attention will be paid to such topics as the unity, catholicity, ministry, and structure of the church. We may add, by way of further preface, that certain emphases described in Chapter II will again be met with here. Some of the familiar refrains will be the following: that the church must be understood in dynamic terms; in relation to its mission; and with its center in Christ. The indecisiveness of the New Testament data with respect to various problems will be asserted repeatedly; and where problems are particularly complex, we will be certain to meet the question, "Is this really an essential element of the matter?"

The Notes of the Church

We turn our attention first to those basic characteristics of the church which are noted in the Nicene Creed – unity, holiness, catholicity, and apostolicity. These are frequently referred to as "marks" of the church. It is more proper, however, to speak of them as "notes" of the church. The marks, then, are those signs by which the church that possesses these notes becomes manifest.[1] Of these four "notes" we shall pay the least attention to holiness, for the simple reason that it has not thus far loomed very large in ecumenical discussions. It may be that "holiness" has not been deemed very important to the subject of ecumenicity. If so, that judgment might well be mistaken. The whole neglected

[1] Charles Westphal, "The Marks of the Church," *ER*, Vol. XII, No. 2, pp. 173-174, 181.

subject of discipline is closely connected with this one; its neglect is a lacuna in the council's theological activities. The other three notes, however – unity, catholicity, and apostolicity – have been clearly seen to have a great deal to do with ecumenicity, and much attention has been given to them.

When one reads the thumbnail definitions of these notes given in the comparative doctrinal statements[2] and elsewhere,[3] he cannot help being impressed by the great degree of similarity between them. The observer might wonder why this aspect of the doctrine should have caused any trouble at all. The fact is, however, that there is a twofold difficulty. On the one hand there are subtle differences that become apparent upon a second reading, and on the other hand the churches have tended to give an interpretation to these definitions that identified the true church with their own organization.

In both of these respects there has been a development toward an understanding of the "notes" that is more dynamic and flexible, and hence more widely applicable throughout the church. One could hardly ask for a more eloquent description of this trend than the following one from a noted Roman Catholic scholar; eloquent not only in its actual words, but in consideration of its ecclesiastical background:

> Once more the *oneness* of the Church is seen as a primarily interior unity of faith and love in the one Holy Spirit who offers harmony simultaneously with freedom. Once more, one sees the *catholicity* of the Church as a catholicity within the variety of the individual Churches, individual opinions, rites, languages, nations, offices, and charismata. Once more, one sees the *holiness* of the Church as a holiness which, borne by sinful men, ever and again requires renewal from the Gospels. Once more, one sees the *apostolicity* of the Church as an apostolicity of the entire community and of its offices in the spirit of the successors of Christ. Few words are needed to make clear the immense significance of all this for the Christian *oikumene* of East and West.[4]

---

[2] R. N. Flew, *The Nature of the Church, passim.*

[3] E. R. Hardy, "The Bounds and Pillars of the Church," *ER*, Vol. XII, No. 2, p. 167.

[4] Hans Küng, *The Structures of the Church* (1964), p. xi.

The dynamic and fluid character of the doctrine is given stability and direction by the fact that every aspect of it is seen in relation to Christ. In each instance the tension between indicative and imperative is present and exercises a formative influence on the doctrine. The church is one, holy, and catholic in Christ, and therefore should be continually striving to be each of these. And it is connected with Christ only through the apostolic witness and so should always be reforming itself back to that witness.[5] There is something very refreshing about these words. They can hardly be taken to indicate a new discovery. What they reflect is principally a rediscovery of something that was genuinely implied and intended in older formulations, but also genuinely lost from view for a while by the churches. The tension between actual and ideal, between already and not yet, between human striving and divine gift, is a very healthy one. And the foundation is the one recommended by the Scriptures as the only one possible (I Cor. 3:11).[6]

Many efforts have been made to illumine the nature of the church further by various formulations. One of the most popular has been the vertical-horizontal schematism. This device, which has been prominent in the movement ever since the First Assembly,[7] is designed to reflect the church's dual character as a divine and a human society. It harmonizes rather well with the already-not yet (or indicative-imperative) motif mentioned above. Not everyone is equally well satisfied with this schematism. One scholar

---

[5] Cf. esp. E. Schlink, *The Coming Christ and the Coming Church,* pp. 105ff. See also *ER,* Vol. I, No. 1, p. 52; Vischer, *A Documentary History of the Faith and Order Movement,* p. 109.

[6] It must be recognized, of course, that this does not solve all problems, because of sharp differences on the person of Christ. These are not obviated, but accentuated by every statement that centers any doctrine in Christ. But it must also be recognized that, as far as it goes, this centralization in Christ is wholly biblical and wholly to be approved.

[7] This continued to be a central emphasis in Visser 't Hooft's address to the Fourth Assembly. Cf. Norman Goodall (ed.), *The Uppsala Report 1968,* pp. 313ff.

speaks of it as a false antithesis, preferring to speak of an eschatological-historical schematism.[8] Another is willing to use the vertical-horizontal terminology, but wishes to insist that even the relation of Christians to each other is really due to their sharing of a vertical relationship to Jesus Christ.[9] Another author has given another generalization that is helpful, in answer to the question where the continuity of the church is to be found. Two traditional answers, he says, are that it is to be found either in the institution and apostolic succession or in the essentials of the faith. He now proposes a new answer, which will transcend the dilemma posed by the traditional two and at the same time do greater justice to the dynamic character of the church's existence. Its continuity would thus be seen to lie in the "unbroken and uninterrupted successiveness of the life of prayer and devotion."[10]

Unity and Catholicity

In the treatment of unity and catholicity that is to follow, it will be impossible to maintain a clear distinction between the two.[11] This is not only due to the close connection between all four of the "notes" of the church. This connection does exist. One writer discusses

> ... the lively way catholicity, unity, holiness and apostolicity are interrelated. Here are overlapping spheres of meaning, master-images that are not mutually exclusive nor fully appreci-

---

[8] William Nicholls, "The Ecumenical Movement and the Doctrine of the Church," *ER,* Vol. IV, No. 1, pp. 30f. One may ask whether "false antithesis" is proper language, since the two were intended to be complementary rather than antithetical.

[9] T. F. Torrance, "What Is the Church?" *ER,* Vol. XI, No. 1, p. 10. "The New Testament word *koinonia* refers primarily to our participation in Christ and only secondarily to our communion with one another in Christ. Primarily it refers then to our union with Jesus Christ, and to such a union that the Church is one body (*synsoma*) with Him, and as such is conform (*synmorphon*) to Him." A similar point is made in the critical remarks by Elizabeth Adler on the address by Visser 't Hooft to the Uppsala Assembly; cf. Kenneth Slack, *Uppsala Report* (1968), p. 27.

[10] Stephen Neill, *The Church and Christian Union,* p. 61.

[11] The Uppsala Assembly had difficulty in keeping this distinction clear. Cf. *The Uppsala Report* 1968, p. 9.

ated apart from each other, that interplay with one another, and doubtless are finally inseparable.[12]

While that interrelation does exist, the overlapping of unity and catholicity is sufficiently great to stand in a class by itself. There are, indeed, aspects of unity and catholicity that are quite distinct from each other. But there is also a broad area in which they appear to be the same thing viewed from different angles.

Taken together, the concern for the unity and the catholicity of the church may well prove to outweigh all the other doctrinal concerns of the World Council of Churches combined. This might seem to be a serious distortion, an imbalance in the doctrinal concern of the ecumenical movement. Such a distortion would exist, and would be serious indeed, if it were really the case that for 60 percent of the time the World Council of Churches were preoccupied with the unity and catholicity of the church to the exclusion of concern for other elements of doctrine. This, however, is by no means the case. The preoccupation of the World Council with the concerns of unity and catholicity is not to the exclusion of other doctrines, but by way of approach to them. This concentration is the occasion for looking at a wide range of doctrines more practically, and hence with a more real and realistic interest, than many of the churches would be inclined to show otherwise. The World Council is not concerned with unity and catholicity alone, but with unity and catholicity as they relate to the whole range of doctrine. A concentration on the unity and the catholicity of the church is the gateway to the search for a joint understanding of all of Christian doctrine by the churches participating in the movement. Nor is this to say that the World Council is not interested in the study of unity or of catholicity in its own right. It is rather to put this study in its proper relationship to other subjects of interest. One might say that their place is found in a hierarchy of interest: unity and catholicity for the sake of the whole round of Christian

[12] Claude Welch, "The Meaning of Catholicity," *ER,* Vol. XVI, No. 1, p. 36.

doctrine; Christian doctrine for the sake of Christian witness; Christian witness for the sake of Christ.[13]

It will not be possible to present, even in summary, all the things that have been said about unity. There would be no end to such a recital, since with only a slight effort everything doctrinal that the movement says may be taken to be related to unity. We shall take up certain important points in other contexts. For example, the important and ever recurring question what kind of unity it is which is sought will be discussed in connection with the structure of the church as well as in other chapters. We shall here content ourselves with presenting and commenting briefly upon the central emphases in the treatment.

Perhaps the most basic of these is that the unity of the Christian church is God's creation and not the achievement of man. There never was a time when the World Council of Churches did not recognize this fact, since it was stated already at the First Assembly in Amsterdam.[14] It is hard to say just where this emphasis had its rise, but it was found clearly expressed in the pre-Amsterdam literature:

> The unity is thus Christ Himself. The messages of Oxford and Edinburgh have this in mind, perhaps, when they say, "The source of unity is not deliberate agreement between men; it is Jesus Christ, Whose Life flows through the whole body, and Who subordinates the will of the many to his own will."[15]

A simplistic response to such an assertion would be to inquire why the churches need exert any effort at all. The ecumenical movement might seem to have no task to pursue, but only a treasure to enjoy. But this would be to short-circuit ecumenical thinking. The church that is properly described as the one, holy, catholic, and apostolic church manifests itself in brokenness. Its unity has now been rediscovered; but the rediscovery creates the demand that the unity be

---

[13] The reader should not attach too much weight to this formulation, which has not appeared in the literature of the movement; but some such description would be in keeping with the actual state of affairs.

[14] Cf. Vischer, *op. cit.,* p. 76.

[15] Ernst Wolf, "Lost Unity?" *ER,* Vol. I, No. 1, p. 52.

expressed. What sort of expression this ought to be is a subject of some debate. It cannot mean monolithic uniformity or institutional centralization. "But neither does the postulate of ecumenical institutionalization allow that the unity which the Church is called to manifest can be reduced to a formal or spiritual unity alone."[16]

A great many words have been written about the manifestation or expression of unity. Not a few of them have been designed to lay to rest the recalcitrant ghost of the superchurch. Particularly from outside the movement there have come persistent warnings that the World Council of Churches was about to become an ecclesiastical monster that would swallow all churches in its ponderous organization. This ghost is indeed a lively one. Its current signs of life will be the object of our scrutiny in the next chapter. At this point it may fairly be said, however, that it would be hard to find any statement in the official or semiofficial utterances of the World Council of Churches that would justify any suspicion that a superchurch with a superbureaucracy staffed by superchurchmen-bureaucrats was in the making. If any blueprint for this exists, it is very well hidden.

The council has enough problems on its hands in the area of unity without taking on any unnecessary ones. When the New Testament is consulted on the nature of unity, the conclusion is reached that "Unity in the Church was not a theological, doctrinal uniformity, but unity in faith."[17] But does not faith seek expression in a formula of some sort? This, it is claimed, was a later development. The original unity of the church is largely mythical. Unity became an ideal in the first few centuries of the Christian era. It developed in both imperial and anti-imperial fashion, but both were developments. In the fourth century:

> . . . among the elements of unity constitutive of the Church on earth we now find elements which seek Church unity essentially within its *structural development;* i.e. the unifying of the

[16] Paul Minear, *Faith and Order Findings,* p. 22.
[17] *Ibid.,* p. 45.

> cultus, of doctrine, of creed, and — supported by a politically constructed centralism — of Church order.[18]

Would it not then be wiser if today everyone should take refuge in an invisible unity of the church? No:

> There is no such thing as an "invisible unity of the Church." There is indeed a spiritual unity of the Church, but no one may with hope of scriptural support claim that no despite is done to this spiritual unity when it does not find visible expression. The *only* unity that the Church has is the unity that she derives from the gift of Christ's glory, and that unity is a unity which the unregenerate *Kosmos,* wholly unattuned to spiritual verities, must be able to *see.*[19]

The Faith and Order Commission moves smoothly from the ground of unity to its expression. Unity belongs to the very nature of the church. Christ alone is the ground of that unity which the Holy Spirit maintains and upholds. The nature of this unity is expressed in the ministry and the sacraments.[20] But there's the rub. It is exactly in the ministry and the sacraments that it has been found impossible to bring the church's unity to anything like adequate expression. It is perhaps a little more hopeful to turn in a slightly different direction and say "that where the Scripture and Baptism are, there is hope of unity, there is already a visible bond of unity."[21] But even this leaves many important questions unanswered. The current state of affairs leaves us pretty much in the position of the writer who described four kinds of unity; the fourth, unity in the ecumenical movement, is real, though it cannot yet find sacramental or liturgical expression.[22]

The World Council's Third Assembly, at New Delhi in 1961, made a great effort to come to grips with the problem

---

[18] E. Wolf, *op. cit.,* p. 51.

[19] Harry R. Boer, "The Glory of Christ and the Unity of the Church," *ER,* Vol. XII, No. 1, p. 20.

[20] Minear, *op. cit.,* p. 46.

[21] Max Thurian, "The Visible Unity of Christians," *ER,* Vol. XIII, No. 3, p. 316.

[22] Gabriel Hebert, "The Church Which Is His Body," *ER,* Vol. IX, No. 2, pp. 115f.

of the expression of unity. The heart of its achievement is found in the following paragraph:

> We believe that the unity which is both God's will and his gift to his Church is being made visible as all in each place who are baptized into Jesus Christ and confess him as Lord and Saviour are brought by the Holy Spirit into one fully committed fellowship, holding the one apostolic faith, preaching the one Gospel, breaking the one bread, joining in common prayer, and having a corporate life reaching out in witness and service to all and who at the same time are united with the whole Christian fellowship in all places and all ages in such wise that ministry and members are accepted by all, and that all can act and speak together as occasion requires for the tasks to which God calls his people.[23]

Comments on this statement have been heard from various quarters. The New Delhi Assembly itself, in the very next paragraph, noted that this statement was far from answering all the questions related to unity. The most significant statement is that "We are not yet of a common mind on the interpretation and the means for achieving the goal we have described."[24] It is therefore recognized that this conception of unity is still a future hope rather than a present reality, and that, for all of its effort to be specific, it still operates in the realm of general theoretical statements.

Another rather pointed comment came from a Roman Catholic adviser at the Uppsala Assembly. Father Roberto Tucci raised the question of New Delhi's "all in each place" in relation to the Toronto declaration that the World Council did not commit itself to any one particular form of unity. New Delhi, he observed, said that unity is visible and organic and excludes a purely spiritual unity. Is this not a "particular conception"?[25] The answer to this must be twofold. On the one hand, the growth of unity must not be overlooked; what the World Council commits itself to in 1961 need not be restricted to what it said in 1950. And

---

23 *The New Delhi Report,* pp. 116ff. Cf. also Vischer, *op. cit.,* pp. 144f.

24 Vischer, *op. cit.,* p. 145.

25 Roberto Tucci, "The Ecumenical Movement, the World Council of Churches, and the Roman Catholic Church" (address to the Uppsala Assembly), *The Uppsala Report 1968,* p. 325.

to avoid the charge of inconsistency it must be added on the other hand that while the council must be neutral in its own organization, it has the perfect right, while observing the proper constitutional safeguards, to point the way toward the unity the churches should seek. That such a development was going on has never been concealed. The General Secretary had written as early as 1955, giving a list of the statements the council had made about unity.[26] The council has gone on record as saying that: the unity of the church is a given unity; it must be made manifest to the world; full unity must be based on a large measure of agreement in doctrine; sacramental communion is a necessary part of full church unity; universally acknowledged ministry and structure of government are necessary, but rigid uniformity and centralized domination are to be avoided; the unity of the church depends upon the renewal of the church; and this unity is not to be sought for its own sake, but for the sake of the world. Whatever restrictions the council may take upon itself, if it is not free to express such conclusions as these, there is no point in its existence.

Uppsala also found occasion to comment on the New Delhi statement. It was recognized that the work of New Delhi had been valuable, but it was also noted that much needed to be done before the ideal there visualized became a practical reality in the life of the churches. "So to the emphasis on 'all in each place' we would now add a fresh understanding of the unity of all Christians in all places."[27]

The comments cited from New Delhi and Uppsala pretty well sum up the matter. The various utterances of the World Council on the subject of unity are solemn and sincere declarations of the intention to find and express and maintain the unity God has given the church. But apart from these, one can find little to choose in actual accomplishment between the member churches of the council and those who

---

[26] W. A. Visser 't Hooft, "Various Meanings of Unity and the Unity Which the World Council of Churches Seeks to Promote," *ER*, Vol. VIII, No. 1, pp. 21f.

[27] *The Uppsala Report 1968,* p. 17.

have thus far chosen not to join. On all sides one finds assent to the fact that there is a spiritual unity of the church which is given by God, that this unity is centered in Christ, and that it ought to come to visible expression. Almost as universal is the agreement that the expression given to this unity is not properly seen as a highly structured institutional unity. The churches have even arrived at this point by somewhat the same road. One may in fairness ask whether the nonmember churches would have been as conscious of the need of unity as they are if it had not been for Faith and Order. Faith and Order activities were probably, to some extent, a positive influence on these churches. Nor is there a great deal to choose between member and nonmember churches when the subject of differences is considered. There are wide and deep differences not only between the two "camps" but within each on other questions than those which have just been mentioned. There certainly is no full agreement as to the boundaries of that church to which God has given His gift of unity, nor on the question of the role to be played in its expression by confessional statements, liturgy, ministry, sacraments, or structure.

But the point to be made here is that neither "ins" nor "outs" have much to show to the world by way of demonstration of this unity. A few small beginnings have been made in church mergers, but where these have crossed confessional lines they have left so many unresolved ambiguities that their leadership remains far from clear. The unity must be made manifest, but it is not. How this stalemate is to be broken is something that cannot yet be seen.

When we turn to the consideration of the catholicity of the church, we find a slightly different situation. There is, if anything, a little less clarity on this subject than there is on unity. But there is a little better demonstration of a growing actual catholicity within the church.

This situation may be due to several factors. It may owe something to the fact that there is not as much pressure to bring catholicity to expression as is the case with unity. Perhaps the expression comes more easily when there is not so much of a conscious effort to bring it about. A growing concept of catholicity may also owe something to the ecumenical movement's practice of trying to include everything that does not defy inclusion. This practice harmonizes well with the notion of catholicity. It may also be due in part to the fact that Protestants had such a long way to go in the development of the concept of catholicity.[28] The very least that can be said of the discussion is that a loose and careless use of the term has come to be sharpened considerably. (There remains, however, a good deal of shoddiness, e.g. in the inability to maintain clear distinctions between catholicity, unity, and ecumenicity.) But in fairness one must say something more than this. The concept of catholicity has begun to come into its own within Protestantism in and through the ecumenical movement. A doctrine to which the churches had long paid little more than lip service has been dusted off and placed in a position of prominence and honor. This fact cannot be negated – though its luster is somewhat dimmed – by the fact that full agreement on details has not yet been reached. Nor is it negated by the fact that full assent can hardly be given to some of the latest emphases. The Uppsala Assembly is a sign both of the negative and positive evaluation. What is said about catholicity is open to criticism. But that so "catholic" a body of Protestants could meet together to discuss this doctrine could not have been imagined in the days prior to the ecumenical movement. This is a measure of the revival of the doctrine of catholicity.

The Amsterdam Assembly perhaps did the cause of clarity something of a disservice by singling out the difference between "catholic" and "protestant" as the deepest difference between its member churches. By this distinction the assembly was not identifying the Roman Catholic Church as over against the heirs of the Reformation. Rather it sought to highlight the differences between those who stressed the visible continuity of the church in the apostolic succession

[28] Cf. V. Borovoy, "The Meaning of Catholicity," *ER*, Vol. XVI, No. 1, pp. 33ff.

of the episcopate as over against those who stressed the initiative of the Word of God and the response of faith, seen especially in justification by faith alone.[29] But this distinction tended to confuse the issues as to what constitutes catholicity and where it is to be found. An article contemporary with the Amsterdam Assembly spoke of the horizontal and vertical ways of understanding the universality of the church. But this did not run exactly parallel with the Amsterdam treatment, since the article identified the horizontal approach with the position of Rome and considered it to be unfavorable to the ecumenical movement; but the vertical approach was said to be characteristic of Orthodoxy, and much more favorable to the ecumenical movement.[30] It was evident that a great deal more clarity was needed in the understanding of catholicity and its bearing on the contemporary life of the church.

Something of that clarity was approached in the succeeding years, partly through the application to catholicity of the same categories that the ecumenical movement has applied to other doctrines. For some reason, perhaps one inherent in the subject itself, this is an area in which the ecumenical effort has been not to narrow, but to broaden the scope of the doctrine. An article that traces the various meanings given to the term in the history of the church notes that it was narrowed to a geographical term by the Roman Church in combat with the Protestants.[31] But it has a wider meaning today.

In an effort to make catholicity more catholic, favorable attention was given to the definition supplied by Cyril of Jerusalem:

> The Church, then, is called catholic because it is spread through the whole world, from one end of the earth to the other, and because it never stops teaching in all its fulness every doctrine that men ought to be brought to know; and that regarding

[29] Vischer, *op. cit.*, p. 76.

[30] Nicholas Berdyaev, "The Unity of Christendom in the Strife Between East and West," *ER*, Vol. I, No. 1, p. 18.

[31] Heinrich Stirnimann, " 'Catholic' and 'Evangelical,' " *ER*, Vol. XVIII, No. 3, pp. 299f.

> things visible and invisible, in heaven and on earth. It is called catholic also because it brings into religious obedience every sort of men, rulers and ruled, learned and simple, and because it is a universal treatment and cure for every kind of sin whether perpetrated by soul or body, and possesses within it every form of virtue that is named, whether it expresses itself in deeds or words or in spiritual graces of every description.[32]

Several emphases now becoming familiar were applied to the catholicity of the church. One writer brought the dynamic emphasis and the indicative-imperative tension into one paragraph:

> However, the view that catholicity cannot be understood merely as a possession, but must rather be regarded as the task of the Church is being increasingly accepted. Catholicity is a dynamic term. The Church of Christ is not merely catholic, but is in the process of becoming so, and the separated churches are bound together in the task of manifesting more fully the gift they have received.[33]

One of his collaborators in this article asserted that there was a relationship between catholicity and both truth and mission, and emphasized the view that the catholicity of the church "reaches toward the maximal and cannot be encompassed in any set of minimum signs."[34] And already fifteen years earlier, the General Secretary had written:

> It is coming more and more to be recognized that this wholeness contains many factors other than the purely intellectual, confessional, and dogmatic. Even our dogmatic convictions are fashioned and modified by our total experience of trying to live as Christians in the light of the revelation of God in Jesus Christ.[35]

As unity came under scrutiny at New Delhi, so catholicity was one of the principal subjects of study at Uppsala. The title of the report adopted at Uppsala was, "The Holy Spirit and the Catholicity of the Church." The dominant impres-

---

[32] Cyril of Jerusalem, *Catechetical Lectures,* XVIII, 23; cited by Welch, "The Meaning of Catholicity," *ER,* Vol. XVI, No. 1, p. 38.

[33] Lukas Vischer, "The Meaning of Catholicity," *ER,* Vol. XVI, No. 1, p. 25.

[34] Welch, *op. cit.,* pp. 39-42.

[35] W. A. Visser 't Hooft, Editorial in *ER,* Vol. I, No. 4, p. 371.

sion that comes to mind when one reads the Uppsala report on catholicity is that it "reaches toward the maximal and cannot be encompassed in any set of minimum signs." This comment is not occasioned mainly by the fact that the report took into its purview unity, holiness, and apostolicity along with catholicity. The striking characteristic of this report was suggested by the Vice Chairman of the reporting section when he introduced the report. "The inward-looking and sometimes even backward-looking conception of catholicity has been radically challenged, and replaced with a forward-looking perspective."[36] In terms of the title of this chapter, the report went to the center and out again to the world.

The report noted with gratitude some real gains in the enjoyment of the gift of catholicity by the churches. But then it went on to note a challenge presented to the church by many observers:

> The Church, they say, should seek its unity through solidarity with those forces in modern life, such as the struggle for racial equality, which are drawing men more closely together, and should give up its concern with patching up its own internal disputes. To this challenge we must listen and make our response.[37]

This was, in fact, the challenge the assembly seemed to confront in all of its activities. The response in this context was to affirm the forward look that the challenge called for, while seeking at the same time not to relinquish the older definitions of catholicity or to "give up its concern with patching up its own disputes." It was recognized that "Catholicity is a gift of the Spirit, but it is also a task, a call, and an engagement."[38] The description of the gift employed some traditional concepts, if not traditional terminology. But the description of the call was less of an old refrain:

> The Church must express this catholicity in its worship by providing a home for all sorts and conditions of men and women; and in its witness and service by working for the realization of

[36] Bishop Karekin Sarkissian in *The Uppsala Report 1968,* p. 7.
[37] *The Uppsala Report 1968,* p. 12.
[38] *Ibid.,* p. 14.

> genuine humanity. The Church hinders the manifestation of its given catholicity when it breaks down at any of these points.[39]

By some observers, this report was highly praised for its forward look. By others it was criticized for a failure to bring into real harmony the two positions it was reflecting. In as far as this was due to the extreme pressures of time under which the assembly was laboring it may, however regrettable, be forgiven. Unfortunately, however, the existence of this real shortcoming leaves unanswered the question whether these two positions can be brought together. This painful uncertainty was felt by some delegates, who held that the traditional view of catholicity had received short shrift.[40]

The questions raised by this attempt at definition of catholicity suggest a comment as to the way this statement was conditioned by its historical context. Whether one considers the timing fortunate or unfortunate depends on his evaluation of the results. But there can be little question that the Uppsala report on catholicity was shaped in large part by the atmosphere that prevailed; an atmosphere expressed by the assertion that the world was writing Uppsala's agenda. The questions to be asked concerning the statements on catholicity are at the same time questions about Uppsala's total response to that situation.

Let us note a few of the questions. Even if one grants the validity and importance of the things said about solidarity with the world, the question remains whether this is a properly designated part of the definition of catholicity. Or has some aspect of mission or witness been rechristened for the sake of novelty? A second question follows from this. What is the relation of this new emphasis to the old emphasis on catholicity? As has been noted, this relation is not clear from the report. Perhaps this emphasis flows consistently and naturally from the emphasis on a dynamic understanding of catholicity; but that connection requires a demonstration that has not been given. And even deeper than this is the

---

39 *Ibid.*, p. 14.

40 See report on discussion, *ibid.*, pp. 9ff.

question whether the new conception can be harmonized with the old. This is by no means a facetious question. The tension between the two emphases in this report suggests a much deeper tension between a traditional conception of the church and a new one that finds the church immersed or lost in the world. Is the vagueness of the language due merely to the fact that the coming reality is not yet fully seen? Or is there about it also a concealment – perhaps unintentional – of a departure from past professions which, however partial or inward-looking, were nonetheless true professions?

Although one might feel uneasy at the open-endedness of the report, it is not easy to bring a rational criticism against it at this point. The struggles of the church to meet new challenges ought to be supported, and not subjected to carping criticism. But there is a nagging impression that the openness is at both ends, the beginning as well as the conclusion. Perhaps the priorities are a bit mixed. Are believers united "in love and service of Christ for the sake of the world"[41] or is the world loved and served for the sake of Christ? One cannot help admiring the cosmic scope of the task visualized in the sixth paragraph of the report. But is it made sufficiently clear that there are conditions of repentance and conversion attached to participation in this catholicity? And if not, how is this catholicity of the church to be distinguished from a worldly catholicity that is opposed not only to the church but to the Christ?

It is too early to judge the effects of this statement. It is too early to know what, if anything, the churches are going to do with it. Nor can one predict whether at some future meeting or in some future study greater harmony will be brought into these clashing fragments. As of the moment, however, one must conclude that the "concentric dogma" has for a time gone past the center and become eccentric. Some correction will have to come in this. Otherwise this effort toward unity will have the effect of being disruptive in the deepest sense of the term.

---

[41] *The Uppsala Report 1968,* p. 13, paragraph 7.

Apostolicity and Ministry

The subject of apostolicity is well suited to the demonstration of both the progress and the problems of the ecumenical movement. Hardly any subject in the whole range of ecumenical discussions lends itself so well to redefinition in terms of dynamism and mission. On the other hand, some aspects of the doctrine have proved to be among the most troublesome in union negotiations. The clash between long-standing and firmly held convictions on the one hand and the attempt to modify these convictions in the interests of unity on the other has provided the movement with one of its most stubborn obstacles. It is because of this situation that the subject of the ministry, which otherwise might well have been treated separately, will be dealt with in connection with that of apostolicity.

The crucial importance of this subject derives from the fact that a given conception of apostolic succession is held in some circles to be essential to the being of the church. All, or at least nearly all, churches hold that apostolicity is one of the notes of the church. But as Bishop Neill puts it:

> On the strict Anglo-Catholic view, episcopacy is of such importance that no group of Christians who have lost or discarded it can claim to form anything that can be called a Church.[42]

The Roman Catholic Church, of course, agrees with this, and this has been one of its chief obstacles in recognizing the ecclesial character of groups of "separated brethren." But on the other hand, the majority of the churches represented in the ecumenical movement have identified apostolicity rather with fidelity to the teaching of the apostles.[43] That the identification of apostolicity has recently moved on to new ground we shall note presently. But this has brought

---

[42] Charles Neill in J. J. Willis, *et al., Towards a United Church 1913-1947,* pp. 136f.

[43] Minear, *Faith and Order Findings,* p. 54. In this instance, the opponents of episcopacy are less comprehensive than the proponents, since the latter say that *both* episcopal ordination and fidelity to apostolic teaching are essential to the church, while the opponents insist that episcopal ordination is definitely not essential.

no easing of the tension involved in this divergence of conviction.

The importance of this problem has been recognized since the early days of the ecumenical movement. This is not surprising, in view of the fact that the Kikuyu Conference had drawn world attention to the problem as early as 1913, and the churches in South India had begun before 1920 to wrestle with it as a prelude to union.[44] The Faith and Order Conference at Edinburgh in 1937 judged that, while differences in ministerial orders were no obstacle to co-operative action, these differences would have to be reconciled before either intercommunion or full corporate union could take place.[45] But the differences have proved hard to reconcile.

All the weapons in the arsenal of the ecumenical movement have been trained on this problem. There has been an attempt to find a compromise formula by declaring that episcopal ordination is not essential, but urging upon non-episcopal churches its value as a sign of the ministry.[46] For many, including many in the Anglican Church, this kind of formula could rather easily be accepted.[47] But for some it would be a compromise indeed; and these include not only defenders of apostolic succession, but also some at the other extreme who still insist that episcopacy is not countenanced by the Scriptures.[48] That kind of opposition is wan-

[44] Willis, *op. cit.*, Parts I and II.

[45] Vischer, *A Documentary History of the Faith and Order Movement*, p. 66.

[46] Minear, *op. cit.*, p. 58.

[47] There is an enormous difference in Anglicanism between the view that the essential thing is continuity with the gospel, of which episcopal succession is the symbol, and that which emphasizes the succession of bishops as the essence of the continuity. Yet the church finds its unity in that it holds the succession, however defined, as the bond. Cf. Dillenberger and Welch, *Protestant Christianity Interpreted Through Its Development*. Cf. also Schlink, *The Coming Christ and the Coming Church*, p. 186.

[48] Apart from those churches opposed to any ordained ministry, the chief opposition to episcopacy has come from the Reformed churches. This opposition is now declining, with most of these churches no longer holding that Presbyterianism is the only warranted form of government in the church. Cf. Flew, *op. cit.*, p. 114.

ing. But with the greatest of willingness to find a compromise formula, there is still no clarity as to how to find one that provides for a new meaning to ordination without implying that the old ordination was substantially deficient.[49] This problem has been the subject of countless negotiating sessions in South India, Canada, and England, and wherever merger discussions between episcopal and nonepiscopal churches have taken place.

The above approach is closely akin to the proposal for a comprehensive ministry put forward by the early Faith and Order conferences. This approach is still being tried, in such merger negotiations as those mentioned above and in the Consultation on Church Union (COCU). What is needed if this approach is to succeed is a shared conviction that this attitude to the ministry is compatible with the New Testament. This would be the case either if it could be demonstrated that the New Testament taught all three forms of the ministry and order, or if it could be agreed that the New Testament teaching marks this as one of the things indifferent to the essence of the church.

It is at this point that two other ecumenical approaches, namely biblical studies and the distinction between essentials and nonessentials, enter the picture. In this instance these two approaches tend to merge into one. If it can be shown that the New Testament does not require a succession of bishops ordained by the apostles, such a succession, however valuable, will be seen to be nonessential. If on the other hand it can be shown that episcopal orders were among those described in the New Testament, then opponents of episcopacy cannot claim that this form of order is not permissible. The appeal to biblical studies and to essential doctrines is, at its best, not an appeal to compromise. It is rather an attempt to allow all that Scripture allows by forbidding only what Scripture forbids.

The general accent of the biblical studies in this area has been on the inconclusiveness of the evidence. Great

[49] Neill, *The Church and Christian Union,* pp. 238f.

obscurity is said to surround such subjects as the process by which the universal priesthood began to express itself in specialized ministries and the identity of the celebrants of the Eucharist in the early congregations. The conclusion is that

> It is probable that there were many varieties of organization in the little communities, as they gradually felt their way to some kind of organized existence. What is quite certain is that none of these forms of Church order was in the least like those which exist in the Churches today; and there is a vast difference between these early and flexible ministries and those which we find in existence in the Church when the obscurity begins to lighten towards the end of the second century.[50]

The special attention of other scholars has been drawn to the question of a specific governmental authority associated with ordination by the apostles. Emil Brunner, consistent with his general emphasis, insists that governmental authority was not part of the apostolic heritage, but was freely bestowed by the Spirit in giving His gifts.[51] And Edmund Schlink teaches that in the New Testament lists of gifts, apostles come early, but gifts of administration are listed late. The special commissioning given in the New Testament was for the work of founding new churches. The New Testament expresses no interest in the chain of laying-on of hands.[52] These scholars do not, of course, speak for the World Council. Nor should it be supposed that there are no defenders of the traditional orders on biblical grounds. But if there is any movement on this question within the ecumenical movement — and there probably is, however slow — it is in this direction.

It may further be mentioned that another ecumenical approach, that of growing together through mutual contact, has worked something of its magic in this respect also. But all of these efforts together have not succeeded in solving

---

50 *Ibid.*, p. 255.

51 Brunner, *Dogmatics:* V, *The Christian Doctrine of the Church, Faith, and the Consummation,* p. 52.

52 Schlink, *The Coming Christ and the Coming Church,* pp. 190, 194, 199.

the problem. The Lund Conference acknowledged far-reaching implications of the doctrine of the ministry. Behind the questions regarding the character of the ministry "lie fundamental problems concerning the nature of grace and the person and work of Christ."[53] This is a reminder that the insistence on episcopacy is not an isolated item of doctrine, but rests upon a conception of the ministry as a priesthood. As one commentator has said:

> I doubt myself the value of plans of reunion like that currently proposed in India which secure episcopal ordination, more or less, but cast doubt on the priestly character of the Ministry of the Word and Sacraments thus constituted.[54]

Progress in this respect has been slow, and some of the heralded breakthroughs of the past have not lived up to their promise. The best that so recent a conference as the New Delhi Assembly (1961) could do was to propose a twofold approach to the reconciliation of diametrically opposite views of the ministry: (1) Rely on the Holy Spirit; (2) continue biblical, theological, and historical studies. The Holy Spirit "will, if we faithfully search, reveal to us the ways in which we can have a ministry accepted by all."[55] One must not, of course, disparage the spirit of *ora et labora*. But the dawn of illumination has yet to break on this subject.

What remains to be seen is whether a tangential development will provide the long-sought solution. This, too, is a familiar ecumenical theme. The ideas of a fresh start and of emphasis on the mission of the church are both implicated in a new definition of apostolicity that is rapidly gaining in favor. When we call this development tangential, we refer only to its relation to the problem of episcopal succession. In and by itself it is a major new development in contemporary thinking on the church and will undoubtedly have far-reaching implications.

---

[53] Vischer, *A Documentary History of the Faith and Order Movement*, p. 109.

[54] Hardy, *op. cit.*, p. 172.

[55] Vischer, *A Documentary History of the Faith and Order Movement*, p. 150.

Although this new development did not receive the full blaze of publicity until the Uppsala Assembly, it was in the process of formation and acceptance for some years prior to that time. The new development is the identification of the apostolicity of the church in terms of mission, either in addition to or as a substitute for the other and older identifications. One might say that to an identification in terms of the office of the apostles, and in terms of their teaching, has been added an identification in terms of their function. More than a decade ago, Weber commented on this development in the *Ecumenical Review* as something that had been in process for some time:

> To be with Christ and to be sent out by Christ — discipleship and mission — together constitute the Church's apostolicity. But throughout the ages only the first element has been emphasized. Many churches have been rediscovering the second constituent element only during recent decades. And symptomatically enough, this rediscovery goes hand in hand with a renewed apprehension of the role of the laity in the life and mission of the Church.[56]

At the Uppsala Assembly, on the occasion of the report on the catholicity of the church, and in the context of a strong tide of orientation to the needs of the world, this new emphasis came to the center of the stage. Uppsala sought not to do injustice to the older definitions of apostolicity, but the accent was definitely on the mission of the church:

> The Church is apostolic in the sense that all that makes the Church the Church is derived from Christ through the apostles. Apostolicity also means the continuous transmission of the Gospel to all men and nations through acts of worship, witness, and human service in the world. The Church is therefore apostolic because she remains true to the faith and mission of the apostles.[57]

It will be seen in the above quotation from the report on catholicity that the view of apostolicity is comprehensive. "All that makes the Church the Church is derived from Christ

---

[56] Hans-Reudi Weber, "The Laity in the Apostolic Church," *ER,* Vol. X, No. 3, p. 288.

[57] *The Uppsala Report 1968,* p. 16.

through the apostles." Teaching, office, sacraments; whatever it is, if it is essential to the being of the church, it comes from Christ through the apostles and is therefore apostolic. But what is singled out for special attention twice in the above quotation is mission.

Uppsala also saw this facet of the church's life in terms of the tension between indicative and imperative:

> The apostolicity of the Church is derived from the Lord's own sending of his apostles to preach the Gospel to all men, yet the Church which in the Christ-given authority of the apostles enters into their mission has not fully achieved her embassy of reconciliation on the world's battlefronts.[58]

And a contemporaneous conference of churches engaged in union discussions produced the statement that "The Church is apostolic in its essential nature, in the sense that it shares in the Mission of the Son by the Father and is empowered by the Holy Spirit."[59]

There can be little question that this interpretation of apostolicity is here to stay. It is not yet clear whether the outcome of its appearance on the scene will be to drive from view the apostolic succession of office and the apostolic succession of teaching, or whether it will share the stage with these interpretations and interpenetrate them. The former is the more unlikely. It would involve a head-on clash with the doctrine of episcopal succession from the apostles, and a clear-cut victory over this long-held position. Such clear-cut victories are rare and are certainly becoming no more common in our undogmatic age. And the entire spirit of the ecumenical movement, as for that matter of all churches in their better moods, is to avoid a head-on clash if possible. And more respectable still is the likelihood that a view that has been so long cherished in the church must have something of permanent validity.

But if the accent is to be on interpenetration, the question still remains how this will be done and how far its effects will go. At present it does not appear that this line of

[58] *Ibid.,* p. 13.
[59] *Midstream,* p. 104.

thought is likely to convince those resolute defenders of episcopal succession who have not already been convinced by other considerations. Nevertheless, it has been demonstrated before that time has a way of subtly wearing away oppositions that seem to be impervious to argument.

The change that is coming about in the definition of apostolicity is a prime example of the trend in ecclesiology today. It is by no means an antibiblical trend. The emphasis on mission is thoroughly in keeping with the original role of the apostles and with the very meaning of the word "apostle." It does appear, however, that it is an untraditional meaning of the long-accepted term. In the ancient tradition of the church an interpretation that connected apostolicity with the office or teaching of the apostles, or both, looms much larger than an emphasis on their being sent out as missionaries. Whatever may be the effect of this change on the old controversies, it is a healthy sign of renewal of vision within the church.

The transition from the discussion of apostolicity to that of the role of the laity in the church is natural and easy. The question of mission and that of the laity overlap at the point of asking, "Who is the responsible agent of evangelism?" The new conception of the church's presence in the world is more and more concerned with the idea that the world will listen to a layman more quickly than to a cleric. This has prompted, or at least assisted, the reconsideration of the tradition that located ministerial responsibility and competence solely among the clergy.[60]

Successive assemblies of the World Council have devoted attention to the role of the laity. The *Evanston Report* notes that the understanding of the church as composed of the laity is in process of rediscovery. Some advance was noted between Amsterdam and Evanston. "The time has come to

---

[60] This tradition has been formally defended in Orthodoxy and Roman Catholicism; cf. N. Afanassieff, "The Ministry of the Laity in the Church," *ER,* Vol. X, No. 3, p. 257. But Protestant churches were no strangers to this position in practice.

make the ministry of the laity explicit, visible, and active in the world."[61] The New Delhi doctrine commonly referred to as "all in each place" was worked out in its practical implications for the local church in what might become a classic blueprint for grass-roots ecumenicity.[62] The New Delhi Assembly stated that "The Church is not the Sunday congregation as we tend to think of it, but the laity scattered abroad in every department of daily life."[63] And the Uppsala report on Renewal in Mission is geared entirely to the concept of lay Christian presence in the world. Clear evidence of this is seen in the section on "Opportunities for Mission," where it is said, "Since the Church is for others, its mission must both challenge and include men and women where they are." The report then goes on to list examples of the opportunities envisaged.[64]

These assembly actions are but the official product of a great deal of writing and discussion on the subject of the laity.[65] The emphasis on the ministry of the members of the church is something to be applauded. It is a revival and further development of a Reformation insight into the priesthood of all believers which was allowed to fall into a large measure of disuse. There are, however, problems both theoretical and practical in implementing this insight. The theoretical problems are found in concentrated form in those communions which have stressed the character of the ministry as a priesthood. Although less acutely, other churches share these problems. It is difficult for most churches not to talk down to the laity. In committees planning a new role for the laity, laymen are often conspicuous by their absence. Some church union documents give high praise to the ministry of the laity and say that no special ministry can ever

---

[61] *The Evanston Report,* pp. 161, 168.

[62] *A Documentary History of the Faith and Order Movement,* pp. 151ff.

[63] *The New Delhi Report,* pp. 88f.

[64] *The Uppsala Report 1968,* p. 30.

[65] Hans-Reudi Weber draws on the Willingen Conference for support for his contention that apostolicity is attached directly to the laity. Weber, *op. cit.,* pp. 286f.

be a substitute for it, and then go on at great length to talk about the problems posed by the special ministries.[66]

But the practical problems are also shared by all churches. In an early issue of the *Ecumenical Review* it was noted that it is difficult to involve "the church at home" in the work of the World Council,[67] and this has been a constant concern of the World Council throughout its years of existence. The crux of the practical problem, however, lies in the fact that this renewed emphasis on the ministry of the laity comes at a time of great uncertainty and confusion in the churches, when memberships are falling off and the interest and participation of members in the church are low and declining. By no stretch of imagination can this be turned into an argument against lay participation. It would much rather be an indication that the attention to this problem is long overdue. But it raises the question, "Where and how are these members to get the inspiration and information for their witness?" Attention to the role of the laity is fine as far as it goes; but without genuine renewal in the church it cannot go far enough. If this is an ecumenical problem, it is so not in the sense of being attached peculiarly to the World Council, but in the sense of being a contemporary problem all Christian churches share. Lay participation may be assisted by programs and structures and encouraged by pronouncements. But it is most likely to come about when there is an irrepressible evangelistic urge welling up from within. This is a frustrating problem for any church organization because its solution is impossible to legislate. Here is a situation where *"ora et labora"* are indeed called for, with the accent on the former.

Before proceeding to consider the means by which the church's unity is to be expressed, we may glance in passing at two subjects related to the above discussion. These are subjects to which the World Council has thus far given only passing attention. It is noted that the ordination of

---

[66] Cf. *Midstream,* p. 112.

[67] Angus Dun, "We Intend to Stay Together," *ER,* Vol. II, No. 3, pp. 267f.

women, which had its earliest prominence on the mission field, is coming to be a major problem among churches seeking unity with each other.[68] This subject was broached at the New Delhi Assembly. But the assembly declined to make a statement on the ordination of women. One of the arguments used was that this was outside the scope of the World Council of Churches.[69] Perhaps that is excuse enough for us, also, to leave it safely to one side.

We find it necessary to pause just a moment longer with the "marks of the church" properly so called. These marks, identified in the confessions of the Reformation age as the true preaching of the Word and the proper administration of the sacraments – with the exercise of discipline sometimes added – have received some attention in the movement, but not a great deal. It seems that the churches are rather well agreed that the Word should be purely preached and the sacraments rightly administered (though even at this point an exception has to be made for those churches which do not recognize sacraments). But not all are agreed on how to preach the Word or how to administer the sacraments. Much unofficial but nevertheless realistic attention has been given to the question how we ought to regard those who differ with us on these points. This involves a consideration of the exercise of discipline, to which the ecumenical movement has given very little attention. The general trend of the movement has been to soften the accent on precision in doctrine, to advocate the permission of wide varieties of approach to the Word and sacraments as fruitful insights, and, in short, to be as comprehensive as possible. This in itself raises a problem of no small dimensions. The accent on comprehensiveness is quite in keeping with the council's role in unifying the churches. In a sense, if the World Council is to succeed in its objective, it will have to reverse a process of mutual unchurching that goes all the way back to the Donatists. But then one might ask what is to stop the council from including the Arians as well? There must be a criterion

[68] Neill, *The Church and Christian Union,* p. 265.
[69] *The New Delhi Report,* p. 217.

of purity somewhere, and some form of discipline to support it. Certainly not all of the former disciplinary criteria could be right. Perhaps this is an indication that they were all wrong. But it will be extremely difficult to find an ecumenical one to take their place.

If Colin Williams is right, as he probably is, the prospect of such a revival of the "marks" is receding, rather than advancing. Speaking of the recognized marks of the church, he says:

> As we have argued, there is real meaning in this emphasis, but it is lack of adequate recognition of the event character of the church that tends to turn it into a legalistic measuring rod which prevents the real question's being asked. That is why . . . "mission" was first added to these marks in ecumenical discussions, leading later to the more radical insistence that the event character of the church must be given primacy.[70]

He comments elsewhere that the Reformers' question and answer are no longer adequate for the church today. They asked, "How can we be sure that the church truly exists within the institution of the church?" And their reply was, "By Word and sacraments." This was adequate in a "Christendom" situation. "But in our exodus situation the question becomes one of *where* the church is the church."[71]

It is one thing to suggest that something has to be added to the position of the Reformers to meet a new situation. It is quite another thing to assume that what they contended for no longer has validity. It is one thing to attack a misuse of this Reformation insight in order to let its real meaning come into view. It is another thing to abandon the insight. In view of the questions raised about existing church structures there is more, not less, reason to stress the need of the church to draw strength from the Word and the sacraments. Rightly understood and practiced, this can only aid mission. If it is abandoned, there can be no future for mission and no missionaries for the future.

---

[70] Williams, *New Directions in Theology: The Church,* p. 80.
[71] *Ibid.,* p. 30.

The Expression of Unity

It is a basic tenet of the ecumenical movement that the unity of the church should come to visible expression. What have been the trends of thinking and what the practical progress in this respect? It is possible to disagree on the very question whether the church is both visible and invisible, and on the meaning of these words. On the former of these questions there has been perhaps less disagreement than might have been expected. In the comparative ecclesiological statements given in *The Nature of the Church,* one communion undertakes to explain and defend the visible-invisible distinction. What emerges from this description is not a great deal different from what is described by the other churches in different terms.[72] It seems that those who repudiate the distinction between visible and invisible largely repudiate something not held by those who maintain that distinction.

But agreement on the existence of the distinction does not guarantee that all agree on the meaning of the words. The Lund Conference addressed itself to this problem:

> We differ in our understanding of the relation of our unity in Christ to the visible, holy, Catholic and Apostolic Church. We are agreed that there are not two Churches, one visible and the other invisible, but one Church which must find visible expression on earth, but we differ in our belief as to whether certain doctrinal, sacramental, and ministerial forms are of the essence of the Church itself. In consequence, we differ in our understanding of the character of the unity of the Church on earth for which we hope.[73]

There is particular unanimity in disavowing the idea that the essence of the church's unity is spiritual and therefore need not come to visible expression. A committee preparing for the Third Conference on Faith and Order was quite emphatic on this score:

> As the incarnate Son of God was truly man, so is the Church wrought out of the stuff of human existence. The Church is

[72] Flew, *The Nature of the Church,* p. 95.

[73] Vischer, *A Documentary History of the Faith and Order Movement,* p. 103.

> shaped in and out of the realities of human historicity and sociality. Therefore the Church is not some "ideal" community, existing in airy abstraction from the affairs of men. Neither is it "spiritual" in the sense that it is to be contrasted with the hard and inevitable materialities of the world of history and sociality. To call the Church ideal or spiritual in those senses is to fall into ecclesiastical docetism akin to the ancient heresy which denied to our Lord his physical body, his historical actuality, his immersion in the stuff of common life. We protest against every view of the Church which in a mistaken effort to exalt its nature as the body of Christ, succeeds only in making it "purer" than its Lord.[74]

There is agreement within the ecumenical movement that the church, and specifically the church in its unity, must be visible to the world. Without such a common objective among the various churches there could be no ecumenical movement. This agreement extends also to churches not in the World Council. It is sometimes suggested that the distinction between member and nonmember churches is to be found at this point: the former emphasize the visible unity of the church, while the latter do not. But this is a gross oversimplification that fails to understand the attitude of many of the nonmember churches.

Although the above committee said that the church "in its concrete expression can be studied as a visible institution subject to the stresses and pressures of the world," it also spoke of the church as a divine fellowship.[75] There are countless other reminders as well of the fact that, while the church is not an "airy abstraction," it is not wholly to be comprehended by sociological measurements. There is a mystery remaining about the church, and part of that mystery is located at the point of the relation between invisible and visible.

> But "appearing," "being manifest," these words do not mean that what is invisible becomes visible; there is still a mystery about the Church. We cannot make the frontiers of the visible communities coincide with the invisible communities of the *Una Sancta,* the body of Christ. We possess no absolute cri-

[74] Minear, *Faith and Order Findings,* p. 24.
[75] *Ibid.,* p. 19.

> terion as to what a true member of the body of Christ is and we are warned in the Bible (Matthew 25:31-46) that there will be some surprises in the day of judgment. We can therefore affirm that our visible communities — however perfect their doctrine, however rich their worship and liturgy — can never be identical with the Church of Christ, but that they are part of it.[76]

While it is being discovered here as elsewhere that mutual study and discussion dispel some of the differences thought to exist, it is also true that the problem of the visibility of the church does not seem to be getting simpler. It remains true, as the Lund Conference stated, that "we differ in our belief as to whether certain doctrinal, sacramental, and ministerial forms are of the essence of the Church itself." It should not be lost from view that a great many differences of profound depth are summed up in that brief statement. And if some growth of understanding and agreement is coming about through mutual discussion, there are on the other hand new issues to take the place of those which are resolved. There is a veritable tide of thinking arising in the church concerning the church's becoming incognito for the sake of penetrating the world. Certainly this is not going to make it easier in the near future to determine what the visibility of the church really is, or even whether it is something to be desired.

If we have correctly discerned the trends within the movement, there is every likelihood that the accent on visibility in the future is to be on dynamic concepts. It will be stressed in some manner that the church becomes manifest in carrying out its mission. What the relation of this to older emphases will be, remains to be seen. In the past it was thought that the visible manifestation of the church should take place in worship, ministry, and perhaps in structure. The question that has yet to receive an answer is whether the new stress on mission will simply be added to the older emphases, or whether it will replace them. The

[76] Roger Mehl, "The Ecclesiological Significance of the World Council of Churches from a Roman Catholic Standpoint," *ER*, Vol. IX, No. 3, p. 245.

answer will depend in part on how successful the former efforts have been. To this question we now turn.

There has been a consistent emphasis on the significance of worship for the expression of unity. The Montreal Conference expressed this quite emphatically. Although these words were intended to refer especially to the unity manifested within denominations, they apply equally to the churches in general:

> All of us would emphasize the presence of the whole Catholic Church in true Christian worship in such ways that there can be no higher unity than that of which we partake around the Lord's Table, and that every other form of unity can only be justified as an expression of that fundamental unity.[77]

It has been vastly more complicated, however, to arrive at a consensus on the extent of unity necessary in worship or the shape that unified worship should take. One of the avenues by which this consensus was pursued was an investigation of the biblical testimony. At least three problems were encountered in this respect. It was found that students from different traditions tended to read the Bible differently.[78] It was also discovered that there was difference of opinion about the sense in which the Bible was authoritative on the subject of worship.[79] And it was concluded that the Bible did not standardize forms of worship and that the tendency to do this is alien to the Bible. It was acknowledged, however, that the great variety of forms the Bible presents all center in the decisive event of the death and resurrection of Jesus Christ.[80]

The concentrated attention given to the subject of worship in preparation for the Montreal Conference produced some interesting attempts at a new approach to the problem of unity in worship. These included one report that was not only unorthodox, but practically incomprehensible in terms

---

77 Rodger and Vischer, *The Fourth World Conference on Faith and Order,* p. 46.

78 Minear, *op. cit.,* pp. 9f.

79 *Ibid.,* p. 34.

80 *Ibid.,* p. 10.

of traditional Christian theology. Among other peculiarities, the compilers of this report preferred to use the term "Being" in place of "God" except in quotations from other sources.[81] In another attempt at a new approach it was suggested that the basic division in worship ought to be designated in terms of "eschatological vs. non-eschatological."[82]

The theme of the church's mission and its relation to worship received its measure of attention. One scholar put the relationship thus:

> As the concentration of God's Heilshandeln, the gathering for worship is the life-giving center of the Church's vital activities in the world. For it is here ever anew that the Lord gathers His people scattered in the world, purifies them from their sins, strengthens them in their temptations, and unites them again with Himself. And it is here ever anew that the Lord sends His people out into the world.[83]

In the meantime, the committees preparing for Montreal found their definition of liturgy also to include something of mission:

> The three activities to which we have insistently drawn attention — professing and proclaiming the faith, worshipping God in the unity of fellowship and faith, and serving the world — constitute the liturgy or reasonable service of the Church.[84]

A unified form of worship, expressing the church's unity, is, however, an elusive object. Appeal to the Bible does not solve the problem, except for enthusiasts for one form or another, and this is no solution. Borrowing left and right from all sorts of forms produces a nonentity with less character than any one of the sources. A grand profession of the beauty existing in diversity begs the question of the expression of unity. Why is it that this diversity exists, and persists in the face of the efforts to dispel it? Undoubtedly a large part of the reason is that different ways of worship involve

---

[81] *Ibid.*, p. 59.
[82] *Ibid.*, p. 51.
[83] Edmund Schlink, "Worship in the Light of Ecumenical Theology," *ER*, Vol. XIII, No. 2, p. 151.
[84] Minear, *op. cit.*, p. 32.

different views of man, of revelation, of the church as ever new event or a continuity in history. The question whether the gospel concentrates on salvation or on the whole of history and life also has its effect on worship.[85] If it is agreed that worship is an authentic expression of what a church is and believes, the churches of the World Council are not yet ready for unified worship, and the history of this struggle is undeniable evidence of that fact.

The persistent absence of complete unity finds its most obvious expression in the movement's difficulties with the problem of intercommunion. Intercommunion is recognized as a most crucial issue in the reconciliation of the churches.[86] Attention is frequently called to the anomaly involved in the fact that the sacrament of unity is the subject of division. This is indeed worth noting. But it arises from the fact that the churches have not yet truly discovered the unity that they believe to exist. They may be willing, on the basis of what they have already brought to light, to engage in other expressions of unity, particularly such theologically innocuous ones as sharing in benevolent work. But they are conscious of not being ready to apply this to the sacrament of communion. However deplorable the division may be, it is to their credit that they do not profess a unity that they do not yet recognize in sufficient detail. It should be added, however, that some individual denominations have solved this problem to their own satisfaction, whether in church mergers or by other means. An outstanding example of fruitful labor on the question of Holy Communion is found in the Arnoldsheim Theses, produced after ten years of conversation among German evangelical leaders.[87]

We come finally to the consideration of the structure (or structures) of the church. It is often assumed that structure is the primary concern of the World Council of Churches,

---

[85] These are among the specific points advanced by Wilhelm Stählin, "Insights and Open Questions Concerning Ways of Worship," *ER*, Vol. IV, No. 3, pp. 246ff.

[86] Minear, *op. cit.*, p. 46.

[87] These theses are reproduced in the *Ecumenical Review*, Vol. XI, No. 2, pp. 188ff.

and that the council aspires some day to incorporate that unified structure in itself. Neither of these assumptions can be uncritically accepted. Nor can they be rejected out of hand. Organizational oneness is not necessarily the goal or even a goal of the World Council. The accepted procedure to date has been that the problems of the structures of a unified church are to be worked out in such concrete union schemes as the union of the Church in South India and the Consultation on Church Union in the United States. Two other possibilities are beginning to become apparent at present. The first is that the World Council will itself embody more of the unified structure than was originally visualized. The second is that all problems of structure will be cast in a radically different light by new developments in theology. We propose to deal with these two possibilities, respectively, in Chapters IV and V.

In the meantime, there are a variety of attitudes to the importance of the structure of the church. In one class of writings this is viewed as a problem of major importance, to which the serious attention of the council must be directed. One study argues that the institutional, administrative, and organizational features of the church have to be rehabilitated. This is not to be done by grafting ecumenical organizations on a pre-ecumenical structure. Rather, a radical new beginning is needed.[88] This is closely akin to the opinion expressed by one of the veteran theologians of the movement. We should, says he, neither acquiesce in the difficulty of arriving at a unified structure nor piece the various structures together by way of compromise. The latter is the worldly way. The new understanding of the Bible must lead to a sounder consensus.[89] Another author is more concrete in his suggestions. Unity should be regional first, with the World Council always holding out the ideal of overall unity. Churches of a congregational polity can never be the basis or even a major constituent part of the structure of a single

---

[88] Ehrenstrom and Muelder, *Institutionalism and Church Unity,* p. 34.
[89] H. Berkhof in *WARC Bulletin,* Vol. VII, No. 4.

ecumenical church.[90] Another well-qualified spokesman notes and takes issue with the Roman Catholic tendency to speak of "the theology (or ecclesiology) of the ecumenical movement." In response to this, he comments:

> As we see it ourselves in the Council, the reality is that we have a fellowship of Churches which have very different theologies and ecclesiologies, which have only begun to enter into closer relationships together, and which cannot therefore have a "theology" or "ecclesiology."[91]

In somewhat of a transitional position, Dr. Mackay notes that the Holy Spirit has not yet revealed the ideal structure of the one church which is Christ's body, and advocates that while the churches wait for this revelation, they should live together in love.[92] There is real difference of opinion, however, as to whether that revelation is to be expected or even desired. The evidence from the New Testament is represented as providing embarrassment not by its paucity but by its abundance. The wealth of definition of church order in the Bible is far greater than could be realized by any one particular church. The doctrine of the ministry must therefore be broad enough to include the various types found in the early church.[93]

Among the denominations there has been a rather general erosion of rigidity on the question of church government. An extreme version of this is found in an article that states:

> In contrast with Rome, we believe that the external structure in no sense describes the inner being of the Church as the assembly of believers. The fact remains that the *Ekklesia* on earth assumes various visible forms. In reality it is not a structure; it merely *possesses* a structure.[94]

---

[90] F. W. Dillistone, *The Structure of the Divine Society* (1951), p. 245.

[91] W. A. Visser 't Hooft, "Notes on Roman Catholic Writings Concerning Ecumenism," *ER,* Vol. VIII, No. 2, pp. 194f.

[92] J. A. Mackay, *Ecumenics, the Science of the Church Universal,* p. 218.

[93] E. Schlink, *The Coming Christ and the Coming Church,* pp. 206, 215.

[94] J. C. G. Kotzé, "The Meaning of Our Unity in Christ," *ER,* Vol. VII, No. 4, p. 324.

But other deductions from the inconclusiveness of biblical evidence and the multiplicity of current forms are more moderate. Form is not considered a matter of indifference, but it should be subordinated to the functioning of the church. Old forms are not lightly to be discarded, but the church must be free to make whatever new ones are necessary to its functioning.[95] Available structures in the church's environment plus the will of God combine to shape the proper structure of the church:

> Of the possible structures at any one time, those are right which effectively fulfill God's intention of saving mankind by the service of a particular people.[96]

This approach was embellished, given particular application, and accorded quasi-official approval by the Uppsala Assembly when it said:

> In this world we need to meet others, across all the frontiers, in new relationships that mean both listening and responding, both giving and receiving. This necessitates:
>
> 1. A continuing re-examination of the structures of church life at all levels, i.e. the local parish, the denominational synods and conferences and their agencies, the councils of churches at national, regional, and world levels. All these must ask, not "Have we the right structures for mission?" but "Are we totally structured for mission? . . ."[97]

One other avenue of approach to the problem is the consideration of the biblical images of the church. This has called forth a considerable literature. We will limit ourselves to a brief comment. The study of biblical images seems well suited to the present mood. How is the church to be understood? Old answers do not suffice. No single church order is discovered in the Bible. But the images may provide the guidance needed to employ a flexible approach with true profit. Different images, however, lend themselves to different emphases, thus raising the danger — always present — that the Bible will be manipulated to support preconceived ideas.

---

[95] Cf. Flew, *op. cit.*, p. 265.
[96] *Midstream*, p. 52.
[97] *The Uppsala Report 1968*, p. 33.

One of the favorite images, which is also perhaps the most prominent one in the New Testament, is that of the Body of Christ. This is recognized as having special importance with respect to unity.[98] But various churches emphasize various biblical images. The Body of Christ is emphasized

> by those who believe the Church to be essentially an organism and institution . . . with its continuity in ministry and liturgical action scrupulously maintained.[99]

An image currently in greater favor is that of the pilgrim people of God. This was accented already at the Faith and Order Conference in Edinburgh, 1937.[100] It is currently receiving renewed attention because of the role it has played in the Second Vatican Council's *Dogmatic Constitution on the Church*. It is considered especially adaptable to the current conception of the church as passing through this world with a minimum of institutional baggage and a maximum of mission. But care must be exercised lest the mission shape the image rather than be shaped by it.

All things considered, it cannot be said that the unity of the church has been successfully demonstrated in the areas of ministry and sacraments. This would not and need not loom so large if it were not for the emphasis the churches put on these aspects of the church's life and the hopes that were entertained for them. If the world is to know of the church's unity by way of ministry and sacraments, the final proof seems almost as remote as ever. The situation leaves many questions unanswered. Will tomorrow bring the breakthrough that did not come yesterday? Has the means for demonstrating unity been wrongly chosen? Is the unity that was to have been demonstrated a reality or a mirage? Ecumenical leaders have long spoken of the pain of divisions. The pain is still there.

The developments we have been considering in this chap-

---

[98] Claude Welch, *The Reality of the Church*, pp. 147f.

[99] J. Robert Nelson, "Many Images of One Church," *ER*, Vol. IX, No. 2, p. 110.

[100] Vischer, *A Documentary History of the Faith and Order Movement*, p. 43.

ter leave the impression of a good deal of unfinished business. There have indeed been some broad lines of growth in the doctrine of the church. But many of the items considered are in flux. The one all-pervading issue which is in doubt is that of the relationship of old convictions to new insights. Can these be harmonized with each other? The question is a crucial one in at least two respects. The unity of the churches in the movement will not be able to withstand interminably the tensions, which are bound to grow if they are not resolved. And the theological soundness of the churches involved in the movement depends upon the interpenetration of old and new. If these are not held together a new schism will result and a new sectarianism will be almost impossible to prevent.

We have concerned ourselves with the doctrine of the church that the ecumenical movement has been in the process of writing. It is hard for an ecclesiastical institution to write systematic theology. It is harder for this institution than for any of its member institutions, because the gap that exists between theologians and churches is multiplied many times over. And it is harder still because the World Council is still a new institution, still uncertain as to its status, without a unified tradition on which to draw, and lacking in sanctions to support its decisions. And yet this is the task in which it has been engaged. Small wonder that the results sometimes leave something to be desired! The wonder is that anything abiding comes out of it at all.

One saving grace is that the council is so willing not only to hear critical things, but to say them of itself. We cannot resist presenting one more quotation, drawn from *The Uppsala Report 1968,* which is published by the World Council itself. It is not, to be sure, a part of that text which was approved by the assembly. It is entitled, "Personal Comment on the Work of the Section on Renewal in Mission." We take the liberty to quote the first paragraph in full, because it sums the matter up in a manner the friendly outside observer might hesitate to imitate:

> There is an almost irresistible urge at ecumenical meetings to produce agreed statements. The milieu, which breathes good will and honest desire for the greatest possible unity, and the pressure of time, combine to embarrass the persistent dissenter, to make him appear and often feel himself ungracious and even obnoxious. Not that there are not spirited, sharp and sometimes prolonged disagreements. There are. But when the record emerges from the drafting committee — where the struggles may have continued even longer than on the floor — the fight is not there. It has been wrapped in the cottonwool of carefully inclusive if not purposefully ambiguous phraseology, or disappears in the safety of well-worn theological platitude. Or the two sides of an issue are stated in widely separated contexts, thus avoiding the necessity of direct confrontation, but resulting in a paper that, read carefully, is less than fully consistent. The statement is finally approved not because anyone is completely happy with it but because everyone can find something, sometimes a great deal, that is very good, and for the sake of this will tolerate what may not be quite so palatable like a guest at a potluck supper. And most are surprised to find that the final result does after all say much of what they hoped for.[101]

A World Council assembly, it appears, is a sort of denominational synod in macrocosm. It may well be thankful for the safeguards built into its own procedures, in the requirement that its decisions be ratified by the member churches before they are binding. And it may well marvel that so much of its work has been as consistent and as abiding as it has proved to be.

Will its present work abide? Some of it undoubtedly will not. But the trends toward dynamism and the emphasis on mission are likely to be with us for quite a while to come. Such permanence is not due to the fact that the council has made doctrinal pronouncements. More likely the council has made the pronouncements because it has discerned that these trends were in the air. Its writing has been descriptive rather than prescriptive.

---

[101] Arne Sovik in *The Uppsala Report 1968,* p. 36. Even more devastating is the remark attributed to Archbishop Fisher, commenting on the Evanston Assembly: "We have done absolutely nothing, and have done it exceedingly well." Quoted in Leeming, *The Churches and the Church,* p. 112.

From one point of view, the World Council is neither to be credited nor blamed for the good or bad developments that are going on. It rides, like the rest of us, on the wave of the times. In the nature of the movement it might have been predicted that it would put the stamp of unity on theology; that theology, including even Church History, would be rewritten with an ecumenical accent. What could not have been predicted was the accent on dynamism and mission, and these are presently taking over the field from the subject of unity.

If that were the whole of the story, it would be useless to register complaints or issue warnings about trends that are more like masters than servants. But while the World Council is engaged in describing what is "happening" it should not and does not limit itself to this. It *should* not, because it is professing to serve the churches in the study of the light shed on events by the Scriptures; and these Scriptures require the church to guard the deposit of faith given to it. The council *is* not merely describing events, because consensus theology is not without influence.

The World Council recognizes this fact. It maintains that its utterances have only the weight that is inherent in them. But it does expect that they will exert some influence. If this were not the case, there would be no point in anyone trying to write theology. We ought just to let it happen. But every believer in divine revelation knows that, at the very least, the Christian canons of interpretation ought to be applied to events, so that they may be understood.

The World Council is engaged in writing consensus theology. This has been its role since the beginning. If consensus theology has any influence, as it certainly has, then it is also dangerous. This need not be merely a general and abstract statement. The danger to which consensus theology leads – whether it be derided as the "least common denominator" or praised as the "highest common factor" – is in the ideas that the truth has no rough edges and that it is determined by majority vote. If unchecked, these dangers must lead theology to the loss of vigor and direction. The more catholic the movement becomes, the more these dangers increase. Faith and Order would have had an easier time if it had been merely a confessional fellowship. When it was joined with Life and Work, language had to be more carefully circumscribed. The same trend was accentuated by the inclusion of the interests of the International Missionary Council, the broadening of the denominational base, the influx of Eastern Orthodox churches, and the increased contact with Rome. A broader base of insight and a wider influence – certainly. But also more positions to satisfy. Everything therefore speaks for vigorous and painstaking discussion before doctrinal pronouncements are made.

The breadth of the base of discussion is commendable, because the problems the council faces are not those of any one segment of the church, but of the church in its entirety. Because of that fact, and because the council welcomes comments from nonmembers, we make bold to comment on two items. The first is the hope that mission will express unity where ministry and sacraments failed to do so. The answer to this seems simple. Mission may express as much, but certainly no more, unity than actually exists. Perhaps it is expected that mission will produce unity. But that is to place the cart before the horse. It may be joyfully discovered in mission that there is more unity than was thought to exist. But unity is at least logically prior. It is the one church with the one gospel that engages in mission.

The other question is that of the center to which the church's doctrine moves. There are many reasons for pursuing this trend. It is a means to the unity of the church. It is healthful for every denomination and every individual Christian to have attention fixed on what is at the center. It is necessary in our times for the church to strip for action to meet the challenge of the day. The World Council is right in pursuing this trend. But such questions as the means to be employed, the distance one should go in relativizing dogma, and the exact location of the "center" must be held in constant scrutiny. Because of its influence, because it is the "great new fact of our time," the ecumenical movement must be scrupulously careful not simply to replace a series of old eccentricities with a new eccentricity.

At the very center is Christ – a statement that has been made dozens of times in ecumenical theology. But let us say it again. At the center is Christ. Not unity and not mission. But do not unity and mission lead to Christ? Yes, if they are correctly understood, rightly used, and properly subordinated to Christ's will, revelation, and purpose. Unity for unity's sake and mission for mission's sake are as vulnerable as dogma for dogma's sake and tradition for tradition's sake. The real center to which unity and mission must lead is the very same as that to which the notes and marks of the church and its ministry and sacraments sought to lead. This is the center that the old formularies and formulations, for all their faults, sought to determine. The fact that they or those who used them confused center with periphery, or tried to pack too much into the center, is not a valid excuse for relocating, abandoning, or ignoring the center.

The church needs a criterion by which to judge when it is passing from the expendable nonessentials to that core of faith which is the true tradition. Again, the official line is the correct one; biblical studies must provide the answer. But again, let it be urged that all subsidiary norms be subjected to this one – dogma, confessions, and traditions; but unity and mission as well.

The World Council of Churches did not create most of the problems with which it wrestles. They are the problems of the church in the world, and any church in the world shares them. The nonmember churches are not only not exempt from the problems; they are not immune to the results, good or bad, of the World Council's struggles with them. All Christians may well seek divine guidance for those Christians joined in this council, and may well speak to them also when occasion arises. If these words of encouragement and warning may do some good, it is sincerely hoped that they will reach their mark.

Chapter Four

THE NEW INSTITUTION

When the Chairman of the Uppsala Assembly made his closing address to the assembly, he called attention to the coming of age of the World Council of Churches. He said,

> . . . there has been constant evidence that the World Council of Churches, established twenty years ago, has now come of age and it begins to face the problems and responsibilities that come when childhood and youth are over.[1]

The fact that the organization had almost reached its twenty-first birthday is the least important aspect of this remark. Far more important is the fact that at the Uppsala Assembly the council was clearly facing a crisis of identity and function. This situation is not radically new; the council has been in some sort of crisis ever since its founding. But it is true with a new intensity and to a new degree. Important questions confront the council at this juncture, and a great deal of its future hinges on which way it will turn at this moment.

Is the council more or less consciously seeking a new role in the life of the churches? It will be the thesis of this chapter that it is, and the objective of the study to discover what that role will be. Some change in direction would be

[1] Norman Goodall (ed.), *The Uppsala Report 1968*, p. 271.

altogether possible and not at all surprising. The World Council of Churches is not the precise heir or copy of any other organization the Christian church has ever witnessed. It has no specific institutional tradition to perpetuate, no pattern of organization to which to conform. In fact, there is no category of church order into which it can be fitted. It is, as it describes itself, an organization *sui generis.*

That in view of such open-endedness some change should come about is rendered inevitable by the pressures on the movement. Although it is incorrect to identify the World Council of Churches with the ecumenical movement, this is often done by outside observers, and frequently by council members themselves. There is good reason for this. The World Council has partaken so fully of the fluid and flexible character of the ecumenical movement that it has often seemed more like a movement than an institution. But in reality it was and is the latter.

The World Council of Churches, as it exists at present, is a composite of many elements. Three of these are movements themselves, each of them having been actively engaged in exploring the field of theology and church life from its beginning. Two of these movements, Faith and Order and Life and Work, came together to form the World Council in 1948. With the third, the International Missionary Council, the World Council maintained always friendly and increasingly close relations until they were merged in 1961. Each of these movements is, in its own way, distinctly forward-looking. But in addition, each has its own emphases and is jealous that its peculiar insights into the matter of Christian unity and service shall be kept alive. Thus there is a constant interaction between these three emphases within the council; and the direction of the council's emphases shifts with the ascendency of one or the other.

A further and rather obvious element in the inevitability of change lies in the official membership of the council. Although the three movements mentioned above have cooperated in calling the council into being, the member bodies are not "movements" or councils of churches, but churches —

or denominations – themselves. It might be expected that an organization composed of denominations would be rather stable and slow to change. But there are elements in the situation that make that result less likely. First, the willingness of denominations to enter into the World Council was in itself an admission that some change was necessary. Second, it was the denominations that were the most ready to make this acknowledgment, by and large, that undertook membership. Third, the composition of that membership has changed during the course of the years; the New Delhi Assembly was a striking instance of that kind of change, when Russian Orthodox on the one hand and Chilean Pentecostalists on the other took up membership in the council. In addition, although this would be difficult to document, it is quite likely that the delegates the denominations send to the meetings of the council, and those who participate in other ways in its work, are among the more adaptable to change among the denomination's members. And finally, these denominations in contact with each other have succeeded in bringing about some changes in each other.

Furthermore, it has been the deliberate and conscious policy of the council to keep a listening ear for the currents of thought, not only in the member denominations as such, but within the environment in general. Whatever may have been the situation in the early years of the council, by this time, in the estimation of some observers, various trends that do not coincide with denominational boundaries have reached a position of major influence. Richard Dickinson included the following as part of his analysis of the Uppsala Assembly:

> In very broad terms, one can generalize that the basic differences in perspective at the Assembly are not between people from different denominations, or even countries or regions, but more directly and noticeably between different age-groups and between high church officials and lower echelons of the Church, and in a most marked way, with lay members.[2]

Add to this the well-publicized desire of Uppsala to listen

[2] Quoted in Kenneth Slack, *Uppsala Report,* p. 8.

to the world, and you have a good indication why change is to be expected.

All that has been said thus far, however, might lead one to expect changes of direction or emphasis within the structure of the World Council of Churches, but not changes in that structure itself. There is another dimension of the council's existence, however, which points to another dimension of the inevitability of change. This consists in its avowed role as the servant of the churches in their progress toward the expression of unity.

This dimension is evident already when only the role of Faith and Order is considered. There is an internal tension between method and objective that is much more productive of movement than of tranquillity. The Faith and Order Movement seeks, by patient theological study, to bring about the reunion of the churches.

> This means that a conservative method has been wedded to a radical vision; this has been the genius of Faith and Order, the basis of its success, and the reason for its continual dynamic.[3]

One might add that it has also been the source of difficulty, that progress has sometimes been slow, and that great waves of impatience sometimes beat on this marriage of method and vision. One might also reflect on the effects of the contacts between the Faith and Order Movement and the Life and Work Movement on each movement. All of this, however, is just a bit beside the point, which is simply that there is an internal tension within the Faith and Order approach that encourages a restless probing for new solutions to the problem of unity.

But what is true of the Faith and Order Movement has also been true of the World Council itself from its very beginning. The council occupied very temporary quarters between the existing denominations and the united church that, however dimly, was visualized for the future. Five years after the founding of the council, Oliver Tomkins reflected upon its position as follows:

---

[3] Keith R. Bridston, "The Future of Faith and Order," *ER,* Vol. XI, No. 3, p. 250.

> We all believe that the Church, which is the Body and Bride of Christ, is something more than our own particular church tradition and yet we all know that we can only *live* daily in the Body of Christ by living faithfully in our own churches. The *status* of the World Council lies in accepting that paradox; its *dynamic* lies in refusing to accept it as final.[4]

The very act of forming a World Council of Churches brought about a change in the relationship of the churches. Without casting any reflections on the undoubted seriousness of the Faith and Order Movement and the Life and Work Movement prior to 1948, it must be said that a new note of seriousness was struck when the World Council was formed. Now instead of merely talking together about how to manifest unity, or merely acting together while waiting for some fuller form of unity to appear, the churches entered into what they called a fellowship. In some degree they were already expressing the beginning of that unity to which they were on the way. Lesslie Newbigin recognizes both the existence of that form of unity and the fact that it cannot be the final form, when he says:

> . . . the World Council . . . is itself a form of that unity. And if the Council be regarded as anything other than a transitory phase of the journey from disunity to unity, it is the *wrong* form.[5]

The churches entered into a covenant with each other at Amsterdam, which carried certain implications with it. Not only did the transition from Faith and Order to World Council spell the end of comparative ecclesiology; it called eventually for the death of the denominations, for new structures to express the new reality; in short, for the expression in the church of the unity the churches profess to have in Christ.[6]

It would be impossible to say how long the founders of the World Council expected it to exist in its original form

---

[4] Oliver S. Tomkins, "Implications of the Ecumenical Movement," *ER*, Vol. V, No. 1, p. 16.

[5] Quoted in Bernard Leeming, *The Churches and the Church*, p. 65.

[6] Tomkins, *op. cit.*, pp. 19ff.

and to function in its original role. This was one of those aspects of the council's existence which was not clear even to those most closely associated with it. But it is fair and significant to say that their fondest hopes for the World Council in that form and that role were that it would not last long. Some other form of unity would emerge soon if the council were successful. What that form would be was not yet known, but it was expected that it would be more perfect and better designed for permanence than the World Council itself. No one can say whether anyone identified that period of temporary existence with twenty years. There is every likelihood that most people at the time thought in terms of slower progress and a longer period of time. But – while some individuals may not have understood or accepted this position – the insistence of the founders from the beginning was that the council was a matchmaker, whose function was to bring the churches together. It was in no way a partner in the marriage itself.

When is that change in role to take place? When is the council, which calls on the denominations to die in order that something better may emerge, going to immolate itself for the same purpose? There are good reasons for saying that the choice must come soon. It may even be argued, as we do propose to argue, that some change has already begun to take place. If this is so, it is all the more urgent reason for the World Council to take stock of itself and consider just what kind of turn of direction is consistent with its purpose.

In preparation for our consideration of change, we must reflect briefly on certain basic tenets of the World Council's position to this date. Of fundamental importance in this connection is the so-called "Toronto Statement." In an effort to clarify some of the issues surrounding the existence of the World Council of Churches, the Central Committee, two years after the founding of the council, received this statement and commended it to the churches for study and comment.[7] This kind of action sometimes administers the kiss of death to a document, but it was not so in this case. The Toronto Statement has achieved a prominence equal to, or perhaps even superior to, the constitution and bylaws of the council. As recently as the New Delhi Assembly in 1961 it was said, "The Toronto Statement still best expresses our understanding of the Council's nature."[8]

This Toronto Statement noted that the Amsterdam Assembly had expressed itself on the subject of the World Council's role in church unity. The council disavowed any intention of becoming a unified church structure independent of the member churches. Its purpose was to express Christian unity in another way. In order to elaborate upon and clarify this "other way" the Toronto Statement first presents a series of five statements as to what the World Council of Churches is not, and then a series of eight statements about the assumptions underlying the World Council. These are all so germane to the present subject that it is hard to select a few for comment. But the following must suffice.

First, it is emphatically stated that the World Council is not and must never become a superchurch. What is meant by this disavowal is made clearer by this excerpt from the attached commentary: "For if the Council should in any way violate its own constitutional principle, that it cannot legislate or act for its member Churches, it would cease to maintain the support of its membership."[9] We underscore particularly the statement that the council cannot legislate or act for its member churches. This is a point to which we will refer again.

The statement proceeds to two declarations that are closely related to each other, although the second of them does not follow immediately upon the first. They are, first:

> 3) The World Council cannot and should not be based on any

---

[7] For this action and the text of the statement, cf. Vischer, *A Documentary History of the Faith and Order Movement,* pp. 167ff.

[8] *The New Delhi Report,* p. 131.

[9] Vischer, *op. cit.,* p. 169.

> one particular conception of the Church. It does not prejudge the ecclesiological problem.[10]

Among the clarifying statements appended to this is the following:

> The World Council exists in order that different Churches may face their differences, and therefore no Church is obliged to change its ecclesiology as a consequence of membership in the World Council.

The second statement reads as follows:

> 4) Membership in the World Council does not imply the acceptance of a specific doctrine concerning the nature of Church unity.[11]

In elaboration of this declaration, various kinds of conceptions of unity are listed. Then it is said:

> But none of these conceptions can be called the ecumenical theory. The whole point of the ecumenical conversation is precisely that all these conceptions enter into dynamic relations with each other.

We shall have to consider whether the council has found it possible to adhere to the position laid down in these statements.

Among the assumptions underlying the World Council, the third is that each church recognizes that the membership of the church of Christ is more inclusive than its own membership.[12] The fourth is that each church need not necessarily regard the other member churches as churches in the true and full sense of the word.[13] The fifth statement in this series is of particular importance, because it suggests that further progress from this point toward unity is to be desired, sought, and expected:

> 5) The member Churches of the World Council recognize in other Churches elements of the true Church. They consider that this mutual recognition obliges them to enter into a serious

---

[10] *Ibid.,* p. 170.
[11] *Ibid.,* p. 171.
[12] *Ibid.,* p. 172.
[13] *Ibid.,* p. 173.

> conversation with each other in the hope that these elements of truth will lead to the recognition of the full truth and to unity based on the full truth.[14]

These utterances present a clear picture of an organization thoroughly committed to the unity of the church, but quite uncommitted to any one theory about that unity. What is particularly clear is that the council is not designed to become the final manifestation of the church's unity. Immediately after the Amsterdam Assembly a pertinent comment was made about the claim made in the basis that the council was "a fellowship of churches." In a description of dialectic tensions at Amsterdam, Dr. Edmund Schlink notes that the World Council is not a *koinonia* in the New Testament sense. The unity that is claimed exists in the face of many continuing difficulties.[15] The disavowal of any aspirations to become a superchurch has been consistently repeated throughout the history of the movement. One of the most uncompromising statements of this attitude was made to the New Delhi Assembly on behalf of the Central Committee by its chairman, the late Franklin Clark Fry:

> ... Without any derogation of the fact, or the slightest lack of appreciation for the blessing, that the Holy Spirit frequently adds a dimension of insight when we act together, there is no question that the churches are the ones that determine the course of the World Council. It, under God and for his purpose, is their servant rather than the opposite. The World Council not only disavowed becoming a "super-church" at its beginning in Amsterdam; its total development since then has been the most convincing refutation of the whole notion. We who are closest to the Council are constantly baffled how any such charge can be made or any such misconception can still exist, except in critics who are deliberately self-deceived.[16]

The World Council, according to its original conception, exists as a service agency, in a sense, of the churches. It serves them in order to bring them into contact with each

---

[14] *Ibid.*, p. 174.

[15] E. Schlink, "The Church and the Churches," *ER*, Vol. I, No. 2, p. 151.

[16] *The New Delhi Report*, pp. 340f.

other, so that they may find the way to their unity. Another description commonly used within the ecumenical movement pictures the present unity of the churches as the gift of God to which inadequate expression is given. The churches are on the way to a fuller expression of the God-given unity. The World Council represents the unity "of the road" that the churches employ in order to progress from inadequate to adequate manifestations of unity. Everything is designed to fit into this picture. Decisions reached by the World Council assemblies are not binding in themselves. They are merely referred to the churches for decision and action. There is, to be sure, a staff and a Central Committee, but the power of these to speak or act for the member churches is carefully circumscribed by the constitution. And the council itself is deliberately designed to work toward its own demise. The true mark of its success would be to discover that the unity toward which it worked had been achieved, and the council itself was no longer necessary.

There are three qualifications that we must make, however, about the clarity and sufficiency of the above position. First, there are some important questions left undefined in the Toronto Statement. Second, there are inherent tensions, which amount to contradictions, within the statement itself. And third, there is an open possibility that later events or riper insights will bring about a substantial departure from the adopted position. We shall be concerned especially with the third of these, but first a word must be said about the other two.

The undefined elements may be dealt with in just a passing word. They represent items of definition that could hardly have been asked of the council at the early stage in its life in which the Toronto Statement was formed. Yet they are important enough to demand clarification as time goes on. One such element is the question what the elements of the true church are and how they are to be recognized in another communion. The peculiarity of the existing situation is that churches are required, as a consequence of membership in the World Council, to refrain from "acts incompatible with brotherly relationships"[17] but not to give up anathematizing one another. Dr. Schlink correctly observes that the council cannot continue to live with these contradictions, but must pass on to what is beyond them.[18] Nor is it clear what are the consequences of membership for confessional positions. One year after adoption of the Toronto Statement, an article in the *Ecumenical Review* commented:

> Ecumenically-minded people commonly say that the ecumenical movement will have implications for our confessional theologies, or indeed for our whole doctrine of the Church. But while it seems likely that this is the case, we cannot begin to discover what these implications are until we clarify the theological nature of the movement itself.[19]

The inherent tension within the Toronto Statement may also be briefly described, although it has proved very difficult to dissolve. It was immediately apparent to some observers. Bishop Newbigin suggested in 1951 that Toronto was just a bit too reassuring. Churches that join the council are not asked to give up their convictions as to the nature of the church. Yet the very existence of the council calls into question the right of separate "Churches" to exist.[20] Eight years later, Keith Bridston attached his critical comments to the statement that "The Council exists to break the deadlock between the Churches."[21] This, he said, appeared to be in contradiction to the assurance that "membership in the World Council does not imply the acceptance of a specific doctrine concerning the nature of church unity" and "therefore no church is obliged to change its ecclesiology as a consequence of membership in the World Council."[22]

We may pass on from these problems because in a real way they are subsumed under the remaining one. We re-

---

17 Vischer, *op. cit.,* p. 175.

18 *The Coming Christ and the Coming Church,* p. 4.

19 William Nicholls, "The Ecumenical Movement and the Doctrine of the Church," *ER,* Vol. IV, No. 1, p. 21.

20 Lesslie Newbigin, "Comments on the Church," *ER,* Vol. III, No. 3, pp. 252f.

21 The Toronto Statement; cf. Vischer, *op. cit.,* p. 176.

22 Bridston, *op. cit.,* p. 253.

ferred to the open possibility that later events or riper insights would bring about a substantial departure from the adopted position. It may well prove to be the case that this has already happened. If this proves to be true in the instance we will now examine, some of the unfinished business will have been completed, and something of the tension resolved, but at the price of raising new problems of consistency.

The instance to which we refer is the New Delhi Assembly's attempt to define the unity of the church. At the least, this definition raises the technical problem of consistency with the Toronto Statement. At a different level, it suggests something with which we will be more deeply concerned, namely the institutionalization of the World Council of Churches. Although we have quoted this statement in an earlier context, we shall do so now again, at greater length, because of its importance to the present discussion. The New Delhi Assembly said:

> We believe that the unity which is both God's will and his gift to his Church is being made visible as all in each place who are baptized into Jesus Christ and confess him as Lord and Saviour are brought by the Holy Spirit into one fully committed fellowship, holding the one apostolic faith, preaching the one Gospel, breaking the one bread, joining in common prayer, and having a corporate life reaching out in witness and service to all, and who at the same time are united with the whole Christian fellowship in all places and all ages in such wise that ministry and members are accepted by all, and that all can act and speak together as occasion requires for the tasks to which God calls his people.
>
> It is for such unity that we believe we must pray and work.
>
> This brief description of our objective leaves many questions unanswered. We are not yet of a common mind on the interpretation and the means of achieving the goal we have described. We are clear that unity does not imply simple uniformity of organization, rite, or expression. We all confess that sinful self-will operates to keep us separated and that in our human ignorance we cannot discern clearly the lines of God's design for the future. But it is our firm hope that through the Holy Spirit God's will as it is witnessed to us in Holy Scripture will be more and more disclosed to us and in us. The achievement of unity will involve nothing less than a death and rebirth

of many forms of church life as we have come to know them. We believe that nothing less costly can finally suffice.[23]

This statement came as no surprise to participants in the ecumenical movement. Something of this sort had been proposed by the Faith and Order Commission a year before the New Delhi Assembly. It occasioned a rash of comment, ranging from outright opposition to firm support. One pole of the reaction is represented by the following comment:

> But this situation throws the challenge that is facing the World Council into sharp relief. The challenge is nothing less than a challenge for the World Council to be truly itself. If the World Council wishes to go on playing its unique and central role in ecumenical affairs, it must not on any account make moves which would forfeit its right to claim absolute neutrality concerning the form the unity of the Church should assume. The World Council must give no pretext for the accusation that it represents one form of ecumenicity, while other organizations represent another. As long as the World Council is prepared to be a meeting ground for any and every form of ecumenicity, it is in a position from which it can offer real leadership to the Church Universal.[24]

Only slightly less critical is the article that asked:

> What would result from the adoption of such a definition of the unity to be achieved? By declaring that we should pray and work for such a unity, would not Faith and Order be leading the World Council into quite a new path — leading it to do what hitherto it has always refused to do, namely to make its own, and officially support, a particular conception of unity?[25]

And in the same article, Dr. Fry was quoted as saying:

> If the new Faith and Order formulation adumbrates, as it may, a new attitude which will tilt the balance toward "churchly unity" and away from consensus of faith, I for one would feel that it ought to be resisted as a breach of the right proportion of things.[26]

---

[23] Vischer, *op. cit.,* pp. 144f.

[24] Lewis S. Mudge, "World Confessionalism and Ecumenical Strategy," *ER,* Vol. XI, No. 4, p. 392.

[25] Henri d'Espine, "The Role of the World Council of Churches in Regard to Unity," *ER,* Vol. XIII, No. 1, p. 15.

[26] *Ibid.,* p. 20.

The latter statement is one of the few that address themselves to the actual content of the proposed declaration. Most of the other negative comments were concerned mainly with the question whether this kind of definition was consistent and proper for the World Council.

As might be suspected from the fact that the statement was later adopted, the consistency of the World Council in making such a statement did not lack defenders. The Bishop of Bristol sought to alleviate the fears of those who thought the World Council might coerce consciences. This would not happen, he said, "so long as any growing consensus of belief about the nature of the Church's unity is the result of a free exchange of convictions within a fellowship."[27] After the passage of the proposal, one author argued that this was really the way of greatest consistency. In framing and approving such a statement, the ecumenical movement is embarked on a way that was implied in Faith and Order from the first, but hindered by the confrontation of diverse traditions.[28] Later comment continued to be favorable. It was noted by one writer that the New Delhi Assembly revised the text of the statement as submitted by the Faith and Order Commission, and he took this as an indication that the statement as adopted had the full weight of the delegates behind it.[29] Several writers noted that, far from being an abrupt development, this action was part of a long process of growing together into a new definition of unity.[30] And finally, the judgment was expressed that this was the only right way to proceed:

> . . . strict ecclesiological neutrality is not possible in ecumenical work. Every joint undertaking demands certain ecclesiological

[27] The Bishop of Bristol, "Legitimate Hopes and Legitimate Fears About the World Council of Churches' Role in Churchly Unity," *ER*, Vol. XII, No. 3, p. 306.

[28] Vilmos Vajta, "Confessional Loyalty and Ecumenicity," *ER*, Vol. XV, No. 1, pp. 33f.

[29] Ernest A. Payne, "Working Out the New Delhi Statement on Unity," *ER*, Vol. XIV, No. 3, pp. 296ff. What does this attitude imply about statements that are adopted *without* revision?

[30] d'Espine, *op. cit.*, p. 19; Paul Verghese, "Will Dialogue Do?" *ER*, Vol. XVIII, No. 1, p. 35.

> presuppositions, and the ecumenical movement would be crippled if certain ecclesiologies could not dominate in certain situations. The attempt must not be to raise cooperation into the void of ecclesiological neutrality.[31]

It would seem that this action was in some sense a departure from the position laid down in the Toronto Statement; but this does not mean that it is to be condemned. It is not a violation of the position adopted in the Toronto Statement, such as would occur if the council should commit itself to, let us say, the congregational or episcopal polity. It is much rather a position that transcends the earlier one. For better or worse, it is the fruit of much ecumenical thinking which has gone on since 1950. While it definitely goes beyond 1950, the churches of the World Council have the right to do this, if they so desire.

The defense of this action does not rest upon the tentativeness of the council's action. Adoption by the New Delhi Assembly meant only, according to the council constitution, that the statement was sent on to the churches for appropriate action. But this is a technicality of little moment. If this were the decisive issue, there would be no point in discussing the case, since no council statement has any more standing than this. The Toronto Statement itself has only that measure of approval. The fact is that statements thus approved are always on tap for future council reference if necessary. What is more significant is that there is apparently no record of any church sending an objection to the next assembly. Presumably, then, those churches which were interested enough to pay attention to the New Delhi statement were in favor of it; or at the very least, not sufficiently incensed to make a protest. It appears that there *was* a consensus and that the churches *did,* in a way, approve. And if the member churches approve what the council decided, who else can deny the council the right to have done so?

What is of considerably greater importance to our purpose is the indication this statement gives of increasing institu-

---

[31] Lukas Vischer, "The World Council of Churches – Fellowship of All Churches," *ER,* Vol. XX, No. 3, p. 235.

tionalization within the World Council. It is, of course, perfectly obvious that the New Delhi statement did not claim that the World Council was a church. But it did commit the World Council to something of an ecclesiology. As one observer has pointed out, this is particularly apparent at the point at which "a ministry . . . accepted by all" is mentioned.[32] The statement is indeed noncommittal at many points. It leaves room for a continuing plurality of denominations, although it does not prescribe that they should remain. In viewing as a thing to be desired "that all can act and speak together as occasion requires," it leaves room for a continuing function for such an organization as the World Council of Churches, although it does not specify that this is the organization that ought so to speak for the "one" church. This statement is commendably flexible at the above points. It is also commendably catholic in its inclusion of communion, prayer, witness, and service, as well as the apostolic faith and the one gospel.

But whether or not this is the best possible ecumenical ecclesiology, and even whether or not it is an acceptable ecclesiology, is not the point. The point is, quite simply, that it is an ecclesiology, to which the World Council is now committed. And committed it is, for the silence of the denominations has indicated their consent. As has been stated earlier, this is not the first time the World Council has committed itself to some aspect or other of ecclesiology. It is, however, probably the most formal and elaborate commitment to date, summing up many of the earlier developments. The recognition of earlier commitments, however, merely underscores the point about institutionalization. The World Council of Churches has had institutional features from the beginning; these increased as time went by; and the New Delhi statement carried them a long step forward.

One of the distinguishing marks of an ecclesiastical institution is that it has a body of doctrine to which it is committed, which it advocates and defends, and by which it is

---

[32] Leonard Hodgson, "Faith and Order's Vision of Unity," *ER*, Vol. XII, No. 3, p. 286.

shaped. This is subtly true even of those denominations which have no formally adopted creeds. The World Council of Churches has made a considerable beginning in the direction of having such a body of doctrine. Those elements of doctrine to which the council is committed probably loom larger in its life than many statements of denominations do in theirs, because the council is a young movement with a cause to advance. Its doctrinal statements are not irrelevant to, or at cross-purposes with, its real life.

It may be said parenthetically that this confronts the "evangelical" critic of the council with something of a dilemma. He may be very insistent in urging that the council should make up its mind on some aspect of doctrine or other. Yet at the very moment that the council does so, there is an upsurge in the threat of the "superchurch" which the evangelical critic abhors. A related dilemma refers to the actual content of the doctrines adopted. It is permissible for critics to urge the council to come to clarity, let us say on the doctrine concerning Scripture and its interpretation. But suppose, as is altogether possible in this imperfect world, that the doctrine upon which the council would agree should be the wrong doctrine in some particular or other; would not this commitment be worse than no specification at all?

As far as the actual content of the New Delhi statement is concerned, the most crucial question is the role of the World Council itself, and, secondarily, the relation of the denominations to the council and to each other. Early in its history, the concept of a permanent world council was subjected to telling criticism. The council seeks to embody "the conviction that the Lord of the Church is God-among-us who continues to gather His children and to build His Church Himself." But the council is not the permanent embodiment of that conviction:

> The more permanent it becomes, the more will it tend to become, in effect, committed to a certain kind of answer to that question. And it will be a wrong answer, because the proper embodiment of that idea is a Church, and not a Council of Churches. Just because the Council is not the Church it will

> become some sort of a monster unless it continually remembers its purely provisional character.[33]

The idea of some sort of permanent council is becoming more and more an open possibility. The changing evaluation of the denominations leaves increasing room for some role for a council for many years to come. Whereas denominations were once looked on in scorn, they are now being thought of as possibly valuable and permanent features of the one church, purged, of course, of their self-centeredness and rivalry with each other. A sociological study of the churches stated:

> Like it or not, denominations have come to mean more than they used to. They exercise wider functions and their functioning is more necessary to the well-being of the local churches than ever before. Denominations increasingly supply the competent planning for their subordinate units and furnish the technical experts.[34]

Another writer entered more deeply into the question of the rightness or wrongness of denominations:

> Denominational existence is not, as is sometimes thought, *per se* incompatible with the New Testament norm of ecclesiological unity; it does in fact become incompatible with it when one part of the body of Christ does not recognize the ministry and sacraments of another. In this sense the New Testament Church was certainly one. In the light of our disruption on this score, it may be said that her unity came to pre-eminent expression in the recognition of the ministry and sacraments of one part by every other part.[35]

The Uppsala Assembly recognized both diversities and the need of limitations upon them, as is evident from the following two paragraphs:

> The quest for catholicity faces us with the question whether we betray God's gift by ignoring the diversities of the Spirit's working. Diversity may be a perversion of catholicity, but often

---

[33] Newbigin, *op. cit.*, p. 253.

[34] Douglass and Brunner, cited in Ehrenstrom and Muelder, *Institutionalism and Church Unity,* p. 361.

[35] Harry R. Boer, "The Glory of Christ and the Unity of the Church," *ER,* Vol. XII, No. 1, pp. 20f.

> it is a genuine expression of the apostolic vocation of the Church. This is illustrated by the New Testament, where through a wide range of doctrinal and liturgical forms, relevant to differing situations, the one unchanging apostolic heritage finds expression. Behind the variety of apostolic activities we discern a double movement: the Church is always "being called out of the world and being sent into the world." . . .
>
> Here we also discern a basis for evaluating the Spirit's gift. A diversity which frustrates the calling and the sending is demonic; the diversities which encourage and enhance the double movement, and therefore enhance catholicity, are of different kinds. . . . By such diversities, intrinsic to the double movement, the Spirit leads us forward on the way to a fully catholic mission and ministry.[36]

It may not be immediately apparent why the greater recognition of diversities, or even the permanence of denominations, enhances the idea of a permanent council. But this becomes clear when one remembers the original objective of the council. The denominations were to cease to exist and unity was to be expressed in one church. The council would assist the denominations to this end; and when the end had been achieved, the council likewise would cease to exist. But if some sort of denominational diversity is to be a permanent or long-range feature of the church's unity, some sort of council will also, presumably, be a continuing feature.

And not only "presumably." The Uppsala Assembly dared to utter a hope that surely would have been considered ecumenical heresy in an earlier age:

> The ecumenical movement helps to enlarge this experience of universality, and its regional councils and its World Council may be regarded as a transitional opportunity for eventually actualizing a truly universal, ecumenical, conciliar form of common life and witness. The members of the World Council of Churches, committed to each other, should work for the time when a genuinely universal council may once more speak for all Christians, and lead the way into the future.[37]

It is not specified that this council should be the World

---

[36] *The Uppsala Report 1968,* p. 15.
[37] *Ibid.,* p. 17.

Council of Churches. It is even said that the World Council's role is transitional. But it is hard to understand what significance that qualification would have. If such a council were to come into existence, speaking for all Christians and leading the way into the future, it would in all likelihood grow in some sense out of the World Council, perpetuate many of its features, and in the nature of the case be called by somewhat the same name. Most likely it would be the differences, rather than the similarities with the present council, which would be incidental.

It ought to be recognized that it is no modest role that Uppsala visualized for the possibly forthcoming council. It is possible to conceive of continuing denominations and a continuing council in quite another way than to have the council "once more speak for all Christians." This alternative conception may be described in terms of "help from the center." There are few denominations, if any, which could not use help from some sort of central organization in meeting the complexities of modern life. The rapidity of change, the shrinking of the modern world, the great demands confronting the church as it becomes conscious of a world role, all tend to make it impossible for denominations to function adequately in isolation. Analogies of this kind of service are to be found in all sorts of international alliances and conferences in business, economics, politics, and military affairs.

The three constituent movements of the World Council had something of this character. Faith and Order, Life and Work, and the International Missionary Council all were designed, in one sense or another, to give advice and assistance to the churches in various aspects of their task. Although this same idea was carried into the World Council at the time of its organization, it no longer had the field to itself. There was a trend toward something more substantial than a service agency. The World Council was an organization of churches, entering into some kind of fellowship with each other. The possibility was thereby created that the World Council would serve somewhat the same function for the denominations as the denominational organizations served for their constituent congregations. But this implies the beginning of a "church."

Although this possibility was officially discountenanced in council statements, the trend of development appears to be in its direction. The alternative possibilities may be described in this way: either the World Council Assembly is a final study committee, passing on the results of its labors to the churches; or it is a "deliberative assembly capable of formulating clear and precise directives" and the "highest legislative body in the Council."[38] In the opinion of one man at least, this is a necessary development at present:

> Whatever may have been the situation twenty or more years ago, it is no longer true that the possibilities of an articulated form of a common faith can be more readily achieved by a Church than by Churches. Now it would often be equally difficult to obtain such an articulation within as between any of the major denominations. All we can hope for is that a common listening to the Word may enable us to move forward together. Confession of faith has become more an ecumenical than a denominational possibility.[39]

It is interesting to note, incidentally, that in exploratory discussions of possible membership in the World Council, Roman Catholic observers have had some difficulty in deciding whether the World Council was a church or not. This is not wholly due to any new ambiguity in the World Council. In part it is due to the ambiguity inherent in the World Council of Churches from the very beginning as an organization *sui generis*. In part it is due also to a natural difficulty that the highly structured and strongly traditional Roman Church has in comprehending a loose, flexible, and novel organization. But the dilemma of the council, between church and nonchurch, is becoming sharper.

The issue of the character of the World Council is one that refuses to be silenced. It is present in the attitude of the "conservative evangelicals" who desire doctrinal clarity on the one hand and fear the superchurch on the other. But

---

[38] Roger Mehl and J. Robert Nelson, "Some Critical Observations," *ER*, Vol. XIV, No. 2, pp. 234, 243.

[39] J. D. McCaughey in *Midstream*, p. 28.

it is also present in churches, both members and nonmembers, who believe that any formulation of position is an infringement on Christian freedom. The latter view came to light clearly in the objections of some churches to the enlargement of the council basis at New Delhi. Neill sees the World Council as a kind of center movement between these two emphases.[40] But that center position is hard to maintain. We have noted the increase in this problem when the churches formed a fellowship at the organization of the World Council. Another straw in the wind was the Montreal Conference on Faith and Order in 1963. It has been noted that after Montreal the Commission on Faith and Order faced a new kind of studies, cutting across denominational lines, such as the Finality of Jesus Christ, Scripture and Tradition, Worship, and the Ministry.[41] This sounds as if the Commission is beginning to serve as the teacher of the churches, instead of merely an agent to bring them together. The implications of this were not lost at the Montreal Conference. One writer comments:

> At least since the Fourth World Conference on Faith and Order in Montreal and the Central Committee meeting in Rochester there has been considerable discussion on what exactly the WCC is. The attempt to clarify the nature of the WCC was soon found to be somewhat disruptive of the fellowship, and has been temporarily suspended.[42]

It would appear, however, that particularly at Uppsala this question has again come into the open.

Our discussion of the World Council trend toward institutionalization has thus far been centered in the adoption of doctrinal positions in general and of a statement on ecclesiology in particular. There are also other indications of a growing institutional character. We now turn briefly to a description of these.

We glance first at the activities of the Central Committee. The very existence of a Central Committee marks an achieve-

---

[40] Neill, *The Church and Christian Union,* p. 370.
[41] *New Delhi to Uppsala,* pp. 55f.
[42] Verghese, *op. cit.,* pp. 36f.

ment of the ecumenical movement. Early in the history of the movement, at the famous Edinburgh Missionary Conference of 1910, the movement achieved an ecumenical breakthrough in the appointment of a continuation committee. This was a marked advance over earlier conferences which had come and gone with little or no continuity. Now it was possible to have the work of the conference go on after it had adjourned. The World Council of Churches has also had, from the beginning, its Central Committee to be its agent and spokesman during the interims between assemblies. But in the nature of the case this committee presupposes the existence of something for which it acts and speaks, and that something is an institution.

One of the most important functions of the Central Committee consists in the issuing of public statements. Ordinarily it is the Assembly itself that speaks for the council. But there are occasions on which a council utterance is deemed necessary between assemblies. When this situation arises, the utterance is either made by the Central Committee or (with rare exceptions) must be approved by this committee before it is published. The constitution does, indeed, make the proviso that any such statement has no weight except what it carries by its own truth or wisdom. But this qualification is widely ignored by the general public, the press, and the critics. And it is to be seriously doubted whether the council or the Central Committee itself are always keenly conscious of it. In the popular estimation, when the Central Committee has spoken, the council has spoken. And when this happens, it is impossible to deny that it is an institution, rather than a movement, which has been heard from.

This feature, as has been noted, was built into the World Council from the beginning. The work of the Central Committee, however, has grown by leaps and bounds. The mere recital of its activities requires page after page of the preparatory materials for each assembly. So large has this work become that it has prompted one close observer to comment:

> From the statement by Chairman Franklin Clark Fry at New Delhi concerning it, the Central Committee's program appeared to have developed into an expression on a large scale of the type of religious activism supposedly particularly characteristic of American churches and long frowned upon in ecumenical circles.[43]

The General Secretary commented upon the tremendous growth in this activity and noted that:

> The churches have become . . . aware of the great resources of the ecumenical movement . . . and are looking increasingly to the World Council . . . to make [these] available to them.[44]

It is not likely that the trend toward increasing activism that came to light already at New Delhi is going to be reversed very soon. To the Faith and Order emphasis and the Life and Work emphasis, which were already in tension with each other within the council, New Delhi added the emphasis of the International Missionary Council, which was incorporated into the World Council as its Division of World Mission and Evangelism. In the light of current thinking about the nature and role of missions, this is most likely to increase the activist trend within the council.

In its activities in the areas of missions and philanthropy, the World Council has sought to maintain the important distinction between direct and indirect activity. Generally speaking, the council does not engage directly in the work of dispensing aid or communicating the gospel. The New Delhi Assembly was at pains to comment on this:

> Although the Division [of Inter-Church Aid, Refugee, and World Service] is worldwide in its outreach, except for certain specialized activities for fostering the welfare of refugees, it is not itself operational, nor has it generally funds of its own to dispense. The Division is rather the co-ordinator between those who wish to initiate projects and those who are able to undergird them in one way or another.[45]

Much the same sort of thing could be said for the mission

[43] David P. Gaines, *The World Council of Churches* (1966), p. 1080.
[44] *Ibid.,* p. 1082.
[45] *New Delhi to Uppsala,* p. 115.

activity that is now part of the World Council. It appears from the report on the Uppsala Assembly that the World Council is now thoroughly committed to a program of Joint Action for Mission (commonly called JAM). This program, involving "redeployment of forces" for mission work, raises vast questions as to the assumptions of the churches participating in it. One would suppose that to commit part of one church's mission mandate to another church implies infinitely more than the recognition of the "vestiges" of the church in the other group. But here again, the World Council is sufficiently sensitive to conscience to emphasize that this is not a centrally planned program.[46] Its commitment to the program takes the shape of encouraging churches to adopt it. For this restraint the council is to be commended. But is there then any point in connecting this mission interest with institutionalism? Yes; the World Council of Churches is the very persuasive institution that encourages its member churches to follow this procedure. In spite of technically pursuing a "hands-off" policy, the council definitely has its hands in the JAM. Whether this is a good program or a bad one – and, given the right conditions, it is very good indeed – the council's measure of involvement in it is a sign that the council is an institution. And in assessing the council's role in interchurch programs it is well to keep in mind the indirect influence of majority opinion. Although the council may not be guilty of any overt coercion, the question still remains whether it puts pressure on a church to soft-pedal its doctrinal emphasis in order to prevent disharmony. And this gives rise to the further question whether such constraint will not produce tensions where they would otherwise not exist.

The World Council of Churches is an institution with a staff. As institutional staffs go, it is small to the point of austerity. But the tendency, as in any flourishing institution, is for the staff to grow.[47] And with growth in staff there

---

[46] *The Uppsala Report 1968,* pp. 233f.

[47] Several new positions were approved by the Uppsala Assembly. See, for instance, *The Uppsala Report 1968,* pp. 197, 205.

comes, in turn, a further growth in institutional character. More specialists, with more of the expertise that is unavailable elsewhere, are present to serve the needs of the churches. Staff involves budget. Again, the annual budget of the World Council of Churches is much smaller than that of many smaller institutions. This is a tribute to the genuineness and determination with which the council leadership opposes the growth of bureaucracy. But the budget requests are growing, and although this is attributed mainly to inflation[48] it is also due in some part to the growing work of the council's staff and committees.

Out of the New Delhi Assembly came a directive to study the changes that ought to be made in the structure of the council. The Central Committee reported to the Uppsala Assembly that this large task had not yet been completed.[49] There is therefore the open possibility that further institutionalization may be forthcoming by the time of the next assembly. The recommendations for change thus far have been unexciting. They have been remedial rather than revolutionary. One of the objectives of the restructuring is to alter the composition of the assembly. It is believed by some that the assemblies are too massive.[50] With over two hundred churches represented in the council, however, it is no small task to reduce the number of delegates while still maintaining adequate representation. It should be remembered, however, that reducing the size of the assemblies will not mean a reduction in institutional character. Rather, it may tend to lay still more emphasis on the work of the permanent staff and the council's committees. While it may make the task of reaching decisions easier, the respective churches will be even less adequately represented than at present. To return to the problem of restructuring the council, it seems unlikely that the very minor changes proposed so far can be the full response to New Delhi's concern about the role of the council. What are the possibilities of future

[48] *The Uppsala Report 1968,* p. 210.
[49] *Ibid.,* p. 281.
[50] Cf. Slack, *op. cit.,* p. 5.

changes? Will the changes proposed for the future satisfy an assembly that goes as far beyond Uppsala as Uppsala went beyond New Delhi? If so, they will have to be sweeping indeed.

When all due allowances have been made for possible, though unintentional, exaggerations and misinterpretations, this recital confirms the truth of Neill's assertion when he said that the World Council of Churches "seems to clothe itself increasingly in churchly garb."[51] That the pressures in this direction are great is undeniable. That the movement in this direction has been as modest as it has been is due in no small part to the real abhorrence of ecclesiastical bureaucracy that is present among the council's leaders. But if an institutionalizing trend persists in spite of resistance, this is all the more reason for the council to be asking itself what the consequences of institutionalization are.

If the institutionalizing trend is to be criticized, it is not because ecclesiastical bodies have no need of change. There is very much to be said for changing structures in order to make them serviceable in the world today. They should, of course, remain true to their essential character, and this is particularly true of churches. But if any church requires structural change in order to serve God better, this is neither wrong nor optional, but ought to be done. This applies as well to the World Council of Churches. The crucial question is not whether any kind of change is permissible, but what kind of change, if any, is necessary to enable the World Council to serve better in its place?

This involves the question, "What is the place of the World Council of Churches?" This is a very complicated question and tremendously difficult to answer. But for our purposes we can simplify it by seeing it in terms of the original conception of the council's role. If any large part of that role remains; if the council is concerned to any substantial degree to provide help to the churches in coming together and in advancing, together, into the future, then institutionalization presents real perils.

---

[51] Neill, *op. cit.*, p. 374.

The heart of the difficulty this presents is in the loss of ability of the council to pursue its vision. True, its original dream has been disappointingly hard to realize. The churches have run into unexpected and unwelcome difficulties in growing together into the one church, as originally visualized. But there are reasons why this should not lead to hasty change. The observation of one Eastern Orthodox observer is correct, that the traditions that have grown over the course of many centuries are not going to be lightly or quickly changed. But it is even more important to inquire into another reason for this slowness to change. Why have the churches not grown together more quickly? An important part of the reason is precisely that they are institutions, with established systems which they wish to maintain and with vested interests which they wish to protect. In that complex of interests there are items good and bad, essential and non-essential; and it is a matter of the greatest difficulty and complexity to sort these out — to "prove all things and hold fast that which is good."

And here is the point. Wherever it may be found, the solution to this problem of the resistance of ecclesiastical institutions to change is certainly not to be found in the erection of an additional institution with its own position to maintain. But this is the peril that opens up before the World Council as it commits itself to an ecclesiology, develops a program, defines points of Christian doctrine, establishes offices, and appoints officers. Building a World Council empire is not a help but a hindrance to building the church of Christ. The ecumenical movement has seen with admirable clarity that the denominations are in constant danger of imposing their will on Christ and of making His church subservient to their church. Not only will the movement serve the churches ill if it does this itself; it must not do anything that interferes with the clarity of that vision or with its freedom to speak that message without fear or favor. It must neither bind its own hands nor compromise its own witness.

Even under the circumstances of its life to date the World

Council has been plagued by the temptation to be mealy-mouthed in the interests of keeping the churches together. This is understandable, but it has serious consequences. Statements wrapped in the cottonwool of ecclesiastical double-talk may serve one aspect of ecumenical interests, but do not serve them all, or serve any of them in the truest and deepest sense. But how certain it would be that this tendency to vagueness in the interests of unity would increase if the council came to look on itself as, in any substantial sense, the church! To the extent that the council ties its hands in institutional red tape, and precommits itself on any issues by its own vested interests, to that extent it breaks faith with its member churches.

There is another and more obvious sense in which becoming an institution is a breach of faith with the member churches. At least since the publication of the Toronto Statement, every church assuming membership in the council has done so under the assurance that it was not committing itself to any particular ecclesiology or relativizing its existence in any way. But the moment the council commits itself to a particular ecclesiology, several things happen. From that moment the council ought to cease advertising the above aspect of the conditions of membership. Whatever may be the outcome for churches already members, no further memberships ought to be accepted under false pretenses. For those churches already members the situation is somewhat different. They had a part (each of them an infinitesimally small part, to be sure) in adopting the policy that has replaced the old one. They have the right of protest if they desire. They have as much freedom as ever to hold over the World Council the threat described in the Toronto Statement: ". . . if the Council should in any way violate its own constitutional principle, that it cannot legislate or act for its member Churches, it would cease to maintain the support of its membership."

But is that threat still realistic? If the council has begun to legislate or act for its member churches, why have none of the churches withdrawn their support? When Uppsala suggested that the churches should work for the time when a genuinely universal council may once more speak for all Christians, why did no church raise an outraged protest? How eloquent is their silence? If silence is eloquent, it is an ambiguous eloquence. How realistic is it to expect objection at this point? When a church has joined with its fellow churches in search for truth, how reasonable is it to expect that church to break that fellowship on the occasion when the fellow churches claim to have found the truth? Is no pressure being put upon the denominations here to muffle their convictions? The group action is all in one direction; any contrary action would be painfully solitary and visible. The issues are all somewhat ambiguous. In short, a great deal has happened to minimize the threat of withdrawal of support. But is that in no sense a breach of faith with those who entered this relationship on the strength of the argument that the threat was a real safeguard?

One may even raise the question how clearly the denominations face the issues raised by World Council policy and practice. The council itself has been disappointed many times that the various denominations seemed to take so little interest and to have so little participation in what it was doing. But the denominations may well counter with a question of their own. How adequately are they represented at council assemblies? The council faces a dilemma here which it would gladly escape. If two hundred member churches are to meet in an assembly of eight hundred delegates, they can have, on the average, only four delegates apiece. What good-sized Protestant church would claim to have been adequately represented by four of its members? The solution might seem to be to increase the total number of delegates. But already the assemblies are so massive that real deliberative action is almost impossible. Due to press of business, the Faith and Order report at Uppsala was not discussed in its final form in plenary session. Complaints about the impossibility of doing business in so big an assembly in so short a time have been heard ever since Evanston. Is it, then, a good suggestion to send only the denomination's "top men"? This would only, in a sense, compound the problem. The proportion of "ecclesiastical top brass" is already so great as to call into question the adequacy of representation. Early in its existence the council decided that about one-third of the delegates to an assembly should be laymen. But such are the problems in working this out that only by very diligent effort has the proportion of laymen been raised to 25 percent by the time of Uppsala.[52] What kind of assembly would result if, on one occasion only, a computer would be allowed to select a true cross section of each denomination for delegation? No true churchman could contemplate that possibility without a nightmare or two. But there is a very real question who is talking when a council assembly announces that "we agree" to this or that. And there is an equally real question whether it can be concluded from a denomination's silence that it is in genuine and positive, conscious and informed, agreement with what an assembly has said.

Our conclusion is that there has been a real departure from the original position of the World Council of Churches. In spite of the emphasis we have laid on the New Delhi definition of church unity – "all in each place" – this is not itself the departure of which we speak. It is a result and a symptom of a broader movement that began much earlier and has continued since New Delhi. This broader movement was potentially present from the beginning of the World Council's life. This potential presence is found in the council's admission that it did not know the shape of the unity that was to emerge from its efforts, in the vagueness and dialectic of the language used to describe the council's role, and in the Toronto Statement's expression of hope that the elements of truth would lead the churches into unity based on the full truth. The accent was laid, however, on a quite

[52] Cf. Slack, *op. cit.*, p. 7; *The Uppsala Report 1968*, p. 191. The percentage is based on the voting delegates. If advisers and observers are included, the proportion of laymen drops. Lay participation at other assemblies is given as follows: Amsterdam, 7 percent; Evanston, 6 percent; New Delhi, 15 percent. Only 14 percent of the delegates at Uppsala were pastors of congregations.

different aspect of the council's role. That this accent has changed is a response to the failure and the success of the World Council. The failure to which we refer is the council's failure to merge the denominations and establish unity in sacraments and ministry. The success is the success of the council in staying together and undertaking activist projects so successful that they have had a mushroom growth. Its failure, seen from a different angle, is the failure to plan effectively for its own demise, and its success that of carving out a more and more permanent and prominent niche for itself.

This development has been accompanied by another very interesting development with which it is deeply intertwined. This is the growth in acceptance of diversity among the churches; or perhaps in ecumenical terms one should say within the church. It is interesting and instructive to consider that something of the same trend, with all of its implications for decentralization, is found in the Roman Catholic Church. Whether in Protestantism or Catholicism, this is partly a genuine insight that can be supported by biblical testimony, and partly a surrender to the tyranny of necessity. It is partly an easy way out of the hard decisions the church has to make as to what is true or false in doctrine, or essential or nonessential in polity. In as far as it is the latter, it is to be viewed with a jaundiced eye.

But in as far as it is a genuine and commendable insight, it raises the question whether the conservatives were not right in the first place; that denominations have their rightful and permanent place, and that the real unity of the church is a spiritual unity. To this the answer of the ecumenical movement would be that it may indeed be true that denominations have their rightful and permanent place. But any recognition of the spiritual unity of the church must immediately be accompanied by the proviso that this unity must become visible. But then the question quickly springs to mind: if the denominations are not going to merge into one church organization, where and how will their spiritual unity be manifest? And the answer that springs as readily into the breach is that the council is the manifestation of that unity. This line of thought ends in making the World Council what it did not want to be – *the* symbol and *the* locale of unity. If that happens, the World Council will have broken faith with itself.

Will this also mean the emergence of the superchurch that the "conservative evangelicals" fear and the World Council disavows? It would be a great deal easier to answer that question if anyone knew just what the superchurch was. This is one of those convenient designations which mean many different things to many different people. All repudiate the superchurch, but each according to his own definition. To one group the superchurch is an ecclesiastical bureaucracy of any size. To another it is an ecclesiastical monster that stamps out doctrinal truth. To a third it is any interference with perfect congregational freedom. And so the opinions go on and on. Whether the coexistence of permanent denominations and a permanent council partakes of the nature of the superchurch depends on the definition, and also on the nature of the relationship between denominations and council. There is a line that must not be crossed, but it is extremely difficult to define that line in concrete terms. The unity ought to be genuine and substantial. The denominations ought to be willing to sacrifice some peculiarities and all prejudices to that unity. But they must never sacrifice principle or compromise the truth. There will be temptations to do so, because they are called to live in genuine and substantial unity with other denominations which, like themselves, may not only be different, but may on occasion be wrong. Where the line of clash between unity and truth comes it is impossible to say. But when unity triumphs over truth, the superchurch has arrived. If the World Council remains true to itself, it cannot represent that superchurch; and if it represents that superchurch, it cannot remain true to itself.

If such a development should ever come about, it would be fatal not only to truth but to unity. For as long as any "vestiges" of the true church remain in that organization, such a development must produce a new schism, or perhaps a new fragmentation into many parts. We cannot but judge that the council's initial instinct was the sound one, and that, in the interests of the unity that it avowedly seeks, it ought to rededicate itself to its temporary, transitional role. Perhaps the goal is a very long way off. But the distance will not be shortened by following a detour.

Chapter Five

THE OBSOLESCENCE OF DOCTRINE

A permanent institutional form is not the only possibility open to the World Council of Churches. It is also possible that there will be a trend of quite a different sort, involving some of the same ingredients, but with a completely different outcome. Instead of the new ecumenical doctrine of the church, this outcome would involve a nondoctrine about what, at least in traditional terms, would have to be called a nonchurch. It would mark the final triumph of those who have thought, over the course of the council's life, that if they only ignored the doctrine of the church long enough, it would go away. The threat of this kind of development is presenting the World Council of Churches with the most serious crisis it has experienced in its entire life.

The factors producing this kind of challenge to the World Council are of many different kinds. Some of them arise from within the movement itself, and some from the outside. Sometimes it is hard to tell whether they are from within or without, and the council does not make this discrimination any easier by its tendency to absorb, adopt, and adapt the latest fads in theological jargon. There is a growing secularization in life, both in Christian and non-Christian lands

— if, indeed, that distinction still has any significance. Neither the World Council of Churches nor Christian theology in general is directly responsible for producing that secularization. But it manages to seep into the council and create a problem. The response to secularization on the part of some theologians has been to formulate a gospel of secularity, which has taken many forms. Part of the World Council's challenge lies in its response to that gospel of secularity. But the reason that this is as serious a problem as it is for the council is that it has an internal tension of its own that now centers on this issue. From the beginning there has been a tug-of-war between the Faith and Order emphasis and that of Life and Work. This can be, and has often been, a very healthy kind of tension, in which both emphases profited from each other, to the enrichment and greater catholicity of the whole movement. But what now threatens is a smashing and final victory for the activist side of this tension, with neither practical nor even theoretical room left for the doctrinal emphases of Faith and Order.

It is at this point that we find the unifying viewpoint for the various subjects that will be treated in this chapter. They are not all of one piece. The evaluation given them may range from hearty endorsement to outright condemnation. But the one element around which they may all be grouped is that they have something to do with the decline of doctrine. They all threaten — though not all with equal intensity and consistency — to render doctrine obsolete and irrelevant. And this remains true whether that doctrine is labeled propositional, or systematic, or biblical, or whatever else.

Thus it comes about that emphases which are good in themselves may be brought into combinations and given an interpretation that will work to the detriment of the World Council. We acknowledge frankly that there is implied in those words a bias regarding the necessity of Christian doctrine. If it should be necessary to draw that implication out into the open, let us state plainly that we consider Christian doctrine to be absolutely essential to the well-being and effective service of the Christian church. And because of the influence that the World Council exerts in the church, we believe further that what works to its detriment is bound to have negative effects on the whole church of Jesus Christ.

Before proceeding to a more particularistic look at the movements referred to, it may be helpful to lend concreteness to some of the above generalizations. How do movements good in themselves combine to threaten the welfare of the church? Social activism has been a basic ingredient of the World Council from the beginning. Despite some persistent criticisms, this is a valid and necessary part of Christian witness. What form it takes, and how it relates to Christian doctrine, determine just how valid any particular expression of it will be. In response to the rise of secularism, however, social activism is reinterpreted in secularist terms, and its relation to Christian doctrine, worked out in interaction with Faith and Order, is ignored or repudiated. It is joined in this by Christian missions, also valid and necessary, but now interpreted in terms of social activism. Because the church, in turn, is interpreted in terms of mission, we find ourselves suddenly at the point where the church is defined wholly by what it does, and what it does bears little resemblance to what it has been doing for nineteen hundred years. It has become the church which is mission / which is social activism / which is a secular presence in the world. There is nothing left of any normative role for Faith and Order. All the latter can do is to try to describe what is going on, at the risk of having even that description repudiated as an irrelevant verbalization. Faith and Order, once a bastion against activist excesses, or in another view a healthy partner in a fruitful marriage with Life and Work, is now in danger of becoming, in activist terms, an organization that merely observes what is happening and explains it for anyone who cares to listen.

The relativizing of doctrine has gone to the point of blurring the distinction between church and world, between Christianity and the non-Christian religions, between faith and atheism. Although we have spoken of relativizing doctrine and of activist excesses in earlier contexts, this is a new question. Now the question has gone beyond asking whether there is to be a World Council of Churches on a more or less permanent basis. Is there to be a Christian church? Is there to be a recognizably Christian presence in the world? We have progressed, if indeed it is progress, from asking whether the Bible is inerrant to asking whether it has any authority at all; from asking who God is to asking whether He is; from bickering with fellow members of the same confession to bland and nonpolemic dialogue with Marxism and atheism.

It is to be noted that we speak of questions. These developments pose questions to the whole church. All churches have to answer them, although not all answer in the same way. For some the answer is so easy that one wonders whether they have wrestled with the problem. For the World Council of Churches the answer is not yet clear. That part of it which has been reached by this time is inconclusive and ambiguous. The answers to be found within the council's orbit do not range all the way from complete repudiation to complete affirmation of the new emphases. But they do range from qualified repudiation to qualified affirmation, and there is a crack between these that will not easily be papered over. The Uppsala Assembly provides all the evidence that is needed for this assertion. To the surprise of some observers and participants, there was no face-to-face confrontation with the "crisis of faith" at Uppsala. There was on the one hand a frequently expressed desire for a more frankly Christian approach to problems. But on the other hand there was a widespread acceptance of the terms of the new secularity which marked a strong trend in the opposite direction.

This is the question that confronts the council. Will it choose for the one side or the other? Or will it seek to comprehend both of these emphases in one organization and one approach? If the latter, which seems by all odds the most likely technique for the council to employ, will it be successful in keeping the two trends in healthy tension with each other? Or will only lip service be paid to one or the other, particularly the emphasis on the doctrinal heritage of the Christian church?

In the following pages we will present our enumeration and description of the issues, together with our evaluation. Our admitted bias in favor of the retention of Christian doctrine is not a complaint against the church entering a new era nor against concern for the world. It is a plea that the church shall not cease to be the church while it makes that pilgrimage and shows that concern. It is a hope that a fruitful tension shall not be resolved by an activist triumphalism. It is a prayer that the name of Christ may be named among all the people of the world. It is a desire that the Word of God shall shine on all of life as its interpreter. This, and not the reverse, is the proper role.

A Recognized Problem

Although responses to this situation differ within the World Council of Churches, there is no lack of awareness of the existence of the problem. If the delegates to the Uppsala Assembly had been in any doubt on this score, this must have been quickly dispelled by the masterful address on "The Mandate of the Ecumenical Movement," by the erstwhile General Secretary, Dr. W. A. Visser 't Hooft. Two excerpts from this memorable speech must serve to delineate his assessment of the problem. He said:

> It seems to me that the present ecumenical situation can only be described in the paradoxical statement that the ecumenical movement has entered into a period of reaping an astonishingly rich harvest, but that precisely at this moment the movement is more seriously called into question than ever before. And once again the basic issue is that of the relation between the Church and the world.[1]

And further:

> Or again, this world needs effective unity. But is the relationship which the churches have in the ecumenical movement more than a pale reflection of the unity they should have? And is the progress toward full unity not so slow that it reveals

[1] *The Uppsala Report 1968*, p. 316.

> rather a fear of unity than a great and passionate conviction about the essential oneness of the people of God? And must we therefore not admit that the ecumenical movement has had its time, and that we have now entered into the "post-ecumenical" age in which Christians will have to make their contribution and render their service to the world through other, less cumbersome channels?[2]

Dr. Visser 't Hooft's response to this situation was a ringing call for a vertical orientation to guide the advance of the church. There have been others who have analyzed the situation with equal clarity but with a somewhat different perspective. In his excellent analysis of the current ecumenical situation, Colin Williams writes:

> It seems clear that [the new ecclesiology] is leading to *a fierce struggle* between those who see [it] as the result of Christ's work in history calling us to new forms of obedience and those who see its departure from the ordered view of the past as a dangerous radicalism that will drain the church of its religious substance and draw the church out of its given spiritual realm into the struggles of the secular world, with the consequent loss of the basic truth the church must offer; that only changed hearts are a remedy for the disorders caused by sin.[3]

As a participant in this struggle, the author is thoroughly familiar with it. His own bias is reflected in the unsympathetic description of the second view in the above quotation. When he addresses himself deliberately to a recommended approach, however, he seeks to hold the two emphases together. After he has described the church in terms of event and institution, and said that these two are always inseparable from each other, but often in tension, he goes on to say:

> Institution is at the service of event, and where the form of the institution is standing in the way of the happening of contemporary obedience to God's call to his people to move on with him in history, then the priority of event must be recognized.[4]

There is little to quarrel with in this. The whole question

---

[2] *Ibid.*, p. 317.

[3] Colin Williams, *New Directions in Theology Today: The Church*, p. 44.

[4] *Ibid.*, p. 28.

hinges on the determination of the point at which institution gets in the way of event.

There are other statements of the matter that are much more extreme, coming from men who do not profess to speak for a settled policy of the World Council, but who seek to bend it to their way of thinking. Three years before Uppsala, Richard Shaull wrote an article that is full of statements like this:

> It is already evident that, as Christians accept their responsibility for building the city of man, they become quite impatient with any ecumenical encounter which consists primarily of academic discussion of differences.[5]

Twenty years before Uppsala, when the World Council was just being born and had not yet "come of age," Karl Barth and Emil Brunner both sounded the note of the church as event, which has echoed and re-echoed in the council edifice ever since. Neither had thought it had anything to do with advocacy of social activism. The event was the meeting of God's people for worship, and particularly the proclamation of the Word of God. But the phrase is coming back to haunt its devotees, for event is now interpreted as a kind of Christian presence that can be neither expressed nor defined by word. It threatens to bring the congregation, that assembly where the event of the church was said to occur, into total eclipse.

The question faced at Uppsala is a classic one for the ecumenical movement. Can the vertical and horizontal be held together? Can concern for the world and concern for the doctrinal heritage be kept in contact with each other, to the mutual correction and instruction of each? Can the World Council continue to be a meeting place of Faith and Order with Life and Work? Can it continue and improve its role of bringing together old and young, lay and clerical? And in order to do this, must it also of necessity be a meeting place of church and world?

---

[5] Richard Shaull, "The Christian World Mission in a Technological Era," *ER,* Vol. XVII, No. 3, p. 213.

The Challenge of Secularity

We turn our attention now to two major challenges that have been presented to the church. Both of them come to the church from outside. Both of them, therefore, have to be faced by all who are concerned for the church's relevance to the modern age. These challenges, which are those of modern secularity and the non-Christian religions, have not loomed as large for all churches as they have for those which are members of the World Council, and particularly for the council itself. This is due to the openness of the council to the issues of the modern age. Insofar as this is expressed in a desire to adopt all current emphases as its own, it is a weakness in the council. But insofar as it marks a readiness to be on the forefront of Christian thinking and action, this openness is commendable and provides services from which all Christian churches may benefit.

Although the challenge of secularity was most unmistakably evident at the Uppsala Assembly, that was not the first time the World Council had shown an awareness of it. More than a decade before Uppsala one writer recognized it as a rival to Christian service in the world:

> Christian *diakonia* will, accordingly, have to accustom itself to the presence in our modern world of this rival religion of brotherhood without God.[6]

And of course it must not be forgotten that secularization had been recognized and highlighted as early as the Jerusalem Conference of the International Missionary Council in 1928. Only at that time it was thought of as the single greatest adversary of the Christian faith. Although that was forty years ago, and these are days of rapid change in theology as well as other areas, the alteration in the attitude toward secularization is nothing short of breathtaking. A tiny suggestion of such a change in attitude is found in another article in the *Ecumenical Review:*

---

[6] T. O. Wedel, "Evangelism's Threefold Witness: Kerygma, Koinonia, Diakonia," *ER*, Vol. IX, No. 3, p. 236.

> The Church can therefore be renewed only by learning to forget itself and to think of the secular world.[7]

But this suggestion is feeble compared with the full-blown advocacy of secularity found six years later. One of the most eloquent spokesmen for the secular judges that the church need not shy away from it at all:

> This need not be a threat to the Christian Church if it is free to understand its own history and the history of its impact upon the western world. *Ekklesia* originally meant an assembly of citizens; in the New Testament, the conception of the Church does not have strong religious connotations.[8]

Responsive members of the younger churches, he goes on to say:

> urgently need to be part of a community of theological reflection and pastoral support in the concrete situation in which they find themselves. As such communities take shape they could become the instruments of decisive Christian participation in building the city of man, as God's purpose for that city is more clearly discerned and the concrete realities of His judgment and mercy are made visible. Out of this might well come a new vision of the shape of the Church as God's people in the new society.[9]

In his article he makes it appear that the establishment of mission schools, hospitals, and other institutions, unrelated to the salvation of souls, was on the right track all along, and that the critics of this activity were dead wrong.[10] This is a sort of self-justification of liberalism, but it goes to lengths that an older liberalism would have hesitated to approach.

The kind of pioneering and experimentation Shaull refers to may be necessary. But then it is all the more necessary for Christians to know with great clarity what it is that they affirm, whom it is that they obey, how He may be known that they may obey Him, and where to rally forces for that obedient service. In other words, doctrine, Christ,

---

[7] Eberhard Müller, "The Structure of Modern Society and the Structure of the Church," *ER*, Vol. XI, No. 2, p. 157.
[8] Shaull, *op. cit.*, p. 208.
[9] *Ibid.*, p. 212.
[10] *Ibid.*, p. 210.

the Bible, and the church are indispensable to such advance. To the credit of the editors of the *Ecumenical Review* it must be said that something of that emphasis was found in the very next article.

The openness to views other than Christianity is reflected in an article in the *Ecumenical Review* written by a Marxist. He advocates dialogue between Christianity and Marxism, claiming that they have a great many interests in common, and that a threat to both of them may make them both able to recognize this fact.[11] This raises all sorts of questions. Must dialogue go on with all kinds of "isms," including atheism, until we see that Christianity is essentially one with all of them? Is this a conceivable ideal for Christianity? Or is it the subversion of the kind of salvation Christ came to establish?

It must not be assumed that every extreme of secularism is shared by every member of the World Council of Churches. This is very far from the actual state of affairs. There is some accommodation to secularization, but here an important distinction is made:

> Swiftly increasing secularization, however, is no less an aspect of the modern scene. Since the IMC Jerusalem meeting in 1928, the churches, which were then proposing to make common cause with other religions against secularism, have been learning to distinguish between the ideology of secularism, which indeed comes under the Apostolic condemnation in the command to "love not the world," and the historical process of secularization, which aims at liberation of the human spirit, and like all other developments of man's potentialities shows the same ambivalence of both good and evil possibilities.[12]

This is a most important distinction indeed. It does not answer all questions. It leaves at least two very practical problems; how is the church to distinguish consistently between the secularization that is to be entertained and the secularism that is to be opposed? And within secularization, how is the

---

[11] Milan Machovec, "Evangelism and Missionary Activity from a Marxist Viewpoint," *ER,* Vol. XX, No. 2, pp. 116ff.

[12] Victor E. Hayward, "The World Council's Fourth Assembly," *ER,* Vol. XIX, No. 1, p. 50.

distinction to be made between the good and evil possibilities? But at least it gives the World Council a place at which to take hold of the problem without necessarily burning its fingers.

The council has been busy in this area. At New Delhi a new cultural consciousness was reflected in the question, "Can the Christian Church be the nucleus around which will be crystallized the culture of tomorrow?"[13] But one cannot help wondering whether the distinctions in terms are always kept in mind. The Jerusalem Conference of 1928 looked on secularism as the enemy *par excellence*. The missions conference at Mexico City in 1963 extended an uncritical welcome to something; was that something the same secularism which was repudiated at Jerusalem? The point to be concerned with is this: if secularization is neither good nor bad in itself, and if secularism is the enemy of Christianity, how are the two to be distinguished from each other?

By the time of the Uppsala Assembly the issue was more sharply drawn, although the outcome was and is not yet clear. There were indications of rising concern with this problem before the assembly met. One writer called on a famous earlier document to indicate that there were some secular forces that were not to be welcomed:

> We repudiate the false teaching that the Church can and must recognize yet other happenings and powers, personalities and truths as divine revelation alongside this one Word of God, as a source of her preaching.[14]

Some theologians had not been content with posing questions to the radical theologians, but had counterattacked. Neill said of Van Leeuwen, Van Buren, and others, "Here we are back in the world of Gnosticism."[15] E. L. Mascall, although by no means an uncritical supporter of the World Council,

[13] *The New Delhi Report,* p. 99. Does this suggest a triumphant twentieth-century *Civitas Dei?*

[14] H. H. Wolf, quoting the *Barmen Declaration,* in "Christ at Work in History," *ER,* Vol. XVIII, No. 1, p. 9.

[15] *The Church and Christian Union,* p. 179.

aided in the evaluation of this challenge to the council when he observed that "Van Buren is interested in secularizing Christians, not in Christianizing secularists."[16] And Karl Rahner contributed the comforting thought that the atrophy of the religious sense may be only a passing phenomenon.[17]

It was felt by some that the battle lines were being drawn in preparation for the Uppsala Assembly. The new General Secretary of the World Council took sides in that battle in a report to the Central Committee published prior to Uppsala:

> It seems to me that it is this widespread modern agreement that there is no transcendent God which threatens most deeply the ecumenical movement. For the movement as we have understood it, has always been Christocentric, and, since New Delhi, explicitly Trinitarian. But the doctrine of the God-Man, of Jesus Christ as the revelation of the transcendent God, can no longer be taken seriously if half of the revelation has neither objective being nor meaning.
>
> Although I am sure that the posture and attitude of the ecumenical movement towards the proponents of "new theological views" must be pastoral and attentive, I believe it to be highly important that we do not give reason to anyone to suppose that we, as a World Council of Churches, are calling into question the being of the God and Father of the Lord Jesus Christ, who is revealed in the Bible to the eye of faith. If this is conservatism and is thought by progressives to be obscurantism, so be it. The ecumenical movement depends today as it has from its beginning on the transcendent God made known in His son, Jesus Christ our Lord.[18]

But the anticipated clash did not take place at Uppsala. The assembly did not give a yes or no answer to either side in the crisis of faith. Both observers and participants gave evidence that a real tension was present, but the issue was handled in such a way that the real outcome is yet to be seen. Kenneth Slack introduces his day-by-day account of the assembly by reflecting on the mounting tensions caused

---

16 E. L. Mascall, *The Secularization of Christianity* (1965), pp. 40ff.

17 Rahner, *Studies in Modern Theology*.

18 Eugene Carson Blake, Report of the General Secretary of the Central Committee, published in *ER*, Vol. XIX, No. 4, p. 449.

by the death-of-God theology, the criticism of the church, the dismissal of the church's doctrine by some and the dismissal by others of its round of activities and forms of worship "as irrelevant to today's secular age."[19] In introducing his more official account of the assembly, Norman Goodall comments that "The most obvious and widely acknowledged feature of the Assembly was its preoccupation – at times, almost, its obsession – with the revolutionary ferment of our time."[20] From the reactions of the delegates it was apparent that some of them thought too much of radical thinking had crept into the various reports of committees and sections:

> It was not surprising that when we met in Uppsala there were protests against too much emphasis on the "secular theology" of Gogarten, Robinson, Hoekendijk, Van Leeuwen, Van Buren, Cox, etc.[21]

Perhaps it was predictable that the Orthodox theologians should have protested "against any tendency to surrender the Christian spiritual tradition to the secularization which was acknowledged to surround all the churches of Europe and America."[22] It might have been expected also that they would have objections to "the participation of the clergy in political and economic pressure groups."[23] But who would have predicted that it would be an American Methodist who would comment on the Report on Renewal in Mission that he "missed any reference to our Lord's command that we are to proclaim the Good News and preach repentance and forgiveness of sins"?[24]

This response from the grass roots – if the rarefied atmosphere of a council assembly can be called grass roots in any reasonable sense – did bring about various modifications in the reports. But it is not yet clear in those reports as modified and rushed through the assembly whether the rival points

[19] Kenneth Slack, *Uppsala Report,* pp. 1f.
[20] *The Uppsala Report 1968,* p. xvii.
[21] David L. Edwards, personal comment on the Section on Worship, in *The Uppsala Report 1968,* p. 83.
[22] *Ibid.,* p. 84.
[23] *Ibid.,* p. 26.
[24] *Ibid.,* p. 25.

of view can be harmonized, or if so, how this is to be done. In part this may be blamed on the insufficient time allowed to an assembly to engage in the kind of discussion necessary for hammering out a meaningful decision. (In this respect the Vatican's years-long assemblies are at an advantage, at least in a formal way.) But there is probably more than a question of available time involved in this indecisive outcome. Even if the time available had been multiplied tenfold, it could not have obviated the fact that this is an issue that cannot be solved by a committee working under a fiat and against a timetable. Nor could it have bypassed the instinctive reluctance of the World Council to adopt any one side of any alternative. It will be necessary for us to study what the World Council is saying and doing to determine what effect the radical theology has had upon it, what reactions this has evoked, and what modifications the council is making in the new theological emphases.

The Challenge of the Non-Christian Religions

But before this is done, we must turn our attention to the description of the second big challenge to ecumenical theology. We refer to the suggestion that the message of Christianity be relativized in the light of the insights of non-Christian religions. We can describe this challenge more briefly, since the issues and the council's reactions are rather similar to those described above.

This issue, which has roots in the comparative religions school of theology, has been present in the ecumenical movement in recognizable form at least since 1937. In that year the question of a *praeparatio evangelica* in the non-Christian religions was debated at the Edinburgh Conference on Faith and Order.[25] In the following year it was found at the very heart of the discussions at the Madras Conference of the International Missionary Council.[26] During the period be-

---

[25] Vischer, *A Documentary History of the Faith and Order Movement*, p. 44.

[26] This occasion called forth Hendrik Kraemer's *The Christian Message in a Non-Christian World* (1938).

tween the Evanston and New Delhi Assemblies, this question came into sharper focus. It was placed on the agenda for discussion at New Delhi. A representative utterance shortly prior to New Delhi indicates something of the nature of the issue and also casts an interesting sidelight on one variety of Christianity:

> ... In Islam there are reflections of the truth and charity which are in Christ. Islam, it is true, rejects the fundamental trinitarian and christological dogmas, but Christ is recognized as Master and Prophet, and, on that point, Islam is not much further from the truth than some Christian liberalism ... we may well ask whether Islam is further removed from Christianity than some Christian sects and heresies. ... Thus the Church is not asked to assume an attitude of conquest but rather one of "presence" and friendship.[27]

One might ask whether that quotation is designed to show how close Islam and Christianity are to each other or how far both are, in their modern versions, from the truth of revelation. But for all that, the quotation puts the issue quite accurately.

The question of the uniqueness of Christianity was a storm center at New Delhi. Its acuteness was accentuated by the dual fact that the assembly was meeting in a Hindu environment and that its main theme was an assertive one: "Jesus Christ, the Light of the World."[28] The assembly was sharply divided over the question of the activities of Christ and the Holy Spirit in the non-Christian religions. The *New Delhi Report* reflects a vigorous argument over some aspects of the report. In what was adopted and sent on to the churches, paragraph 17 is a completely rewritten version of what was earlier submitted for adoption.[29] Nevertheless it is still something on which the assembly had to reflect a divided

---

[27] Max Thurian, "The Visible Unity of Christians," *ER,* Vol. XIII, No. 3, p. 315.

[28] This juxtaposition elicted caustic comment from some delegates; cf. David Gaines, *The World Council of Churches: A Study of Its Background and History,* pp. 1071f.

[29] *The New Delhi Report,* pp. 48, 70.

mind. It was decided that this was a subject that required further study.

A small reflection of the way thinking had changed since the publication in 1938 of Hendrik Kraemer's *The Christian Message in a Non-Christian World* is given in an article appearing shortly after New Delhi. It said in part:

> The idea of a "non-Christian world" of religions and cultures from which Christ's presence and power are excluded dies hard. In the present period of history there is no religion or culture which has not heard the gospel of Jesus Christ or acknowledged its power through positive response and/or hostility to him. It is no longer the "Christian message in a non-Christian world" that we have to discuss, but the relation between "the Word of God and the Living Faiths of Men," not primarily the relation between Christian and non-Christian systems of thought and life but between men of different faiths all standing under the judging and redeeming word of God.[30]

The situation was not greatly clarified at Uppsala. H. Berkhof addressed the assembly on "The Finality of Jesus Christ: our common confession and its implications for today."[31] In his estimation, his subject had bearing on both of the challenges we are considering: the "age-old world of the great religions" and the "modern secularized world." This twofold denial of the finality of Christ "comes not only from outside" but "resounds in the hearts of innumerable Christians."[32] The speaker roundly affirmed the finality of Jesus Christ, grounding it in Christ's resurrection from the dead.[33] But in the brief report on the discussion of this address there are signs that the basic difference of opinion still remains.[34]

The fact that the finality of Jesus Christ is called into question is not due to any lack of defenders from among the ecumenical ranks. Visser 't Hooft led the defense of the

---

[30] M. M. Thomas, "Some Critical Observations," *ER*, Vol. XIV, No. 2, p. 248.

[31] *The Uppsala Report 1968*, p. 116.

[32] *Ibid.*, p. 305.

[33] *Ibid.*, p. 306.

[34] *Ibid.*, p. 116. Is revelation "the openness of men to all reality" or an "event which ceased with the death and resurrection of Jesus Christ"?

finality of Christ with his masterful little book, *No Other Name*.[35] It is, in fact, the very excellence of the defenses of Christ's finality that makes the continuing opposition to it so ominous. The questions do not disappear in the face of a vigorous and eloquent defense. This is a sign that the approaches to theology through comparative religions and direct divine revelation are poles apart. Neither party to this dispute is likely to think of its difference from the other as something minor or nonessential. Comprehending the two views in one organization is logically impossible, however ecumenically possible it may be. This is far from being a simple matter of deciding whether or not Christians should approach other men with chips on their shoulders. Nor is it merely a matter of learning some new insight from the closer study of other religions. The question whether Jesus Christ is the unique revelation of the Father is not a mere matter of technique, does not lend itself to compromise, and provides an issue on which the World Council will have to decide which direction it will take.

The depth of this issue is seen even more clearly if we take seriously the above quotation from the article by Max Thurian. If "we may well ask whether Islam is further removed from Christianity than some Christian sects and heresies," then we may have to ask other questions as well. The World Council may well begin asking whether it has set the bounds of the church and those of its own organization at the right places. Must it open its doors to Islam, Hinduism, Marxism, and atheism? Or will it presently discover that it is necessary to draw the church/nonchurch line at this point of the recognition of Christ's finality? Is this issue negotiable, or is it not?

Varieties of Response: Social Activism

We turn now to a consideration of the varieties of response within the World Council to this great new challenge. The council has long been concerned with the definition

[35] W. A. Visser 't Hooft, *No Other Name: The Choice Between Syncretism and Christian Universalism* (1963).

of unity and the role of the council itself in that unity. Although those questions still remain, the inquiry has moved beyond them. The debate today is more concerned with these questions: what is church and what is nonchurch? What is world, what is gospel, what is witness, what is mission? The council, and for that matter the whole church, is facing the challenge of a revolutionary age that has questioned old certainties in every aspect of life.

The story would be simpler if the World Council of Churches had either wholly endorsed or flatly opposed this questioning trend. This the council has not done; whether it is to be blamed for this is another question. The simplest answer is not always the best. If the church is to give satisfactory answers to any questions, it has to face those questions seriously. It is to the credit of the council, whatever one may say of the outcome, that it has sought to face the questions in depth, and not avoided them by the repetition of clichés. An examination of the council's actions faces us rather with a variety of positive responses to the new questions. Each of these carries its own tensions within itself. Each therefore leaves the final answer to the subsidiary questions and the main question unclear. If we are to find any basis for evaluation, it will have to be concerned with degrees of affirmation or negation and with relative emphases on the eternal truths and the changing circumstances. It is in these that the evaluations made by the council come to light, and we shall have to evaluate that evaluation.

The first area of response is social activism. In this area the current trend is a sharp accentuation of a long-standing element in the council's program. It is actually older in the ecumenical movement than the concern for clarity and unity on questions of doctrine. It has been considerably easier for the council to achieve a measure of unity in this respect than in doctrine. The programs, as a consequence, have multiplied and expanded. The easiest area of all appears to be that of interchurch aid and social service. By contrast with such areas as missions and education, the activity here is less restricted to consultation and advice.[36] There are three levels or aspects of contact through Inter-Church Aid. They vary in directness, but include direct action by the division on behalf of the churches. The division is careful, however, to work through the churches wherever possible.[37]

Far from declining, this activity took a sharp upturn at the Uppsala Assembly. Perhaps this is a reflection of the "tendency of youth everywhere (supported by many adults) to give up on all organizations and support only movements."[38] It has been noted that the Uppsala Assembly was preoccupied

> with the revolutionary ferment of our time, with questions of social and international responsibility, of war and peace, and economic justice, with the pressing, agonizing physical needs of men, with the plight of the underprivileged, the homeless and starving, and with the most radical contemporary rebellions against all "establishments," civil and religious.[39]

This was the church newly conscious of the world, and looking outward from itself on the world.

Further details need not be given, because the question of evaluation can be faced at this point. For some the evaluation is not far to seek. For those who believe that nothing of this sort is any business of the church, who have been suspicious of socialist overtones in World Council activism from the start,[40] this is the final and conclusive demonstration of the fact that the council is on the wrong track. The Geneva Conference on Church and Society, they would say, was bad enough; but now the possibility of arguing that Geneva did not speak for the World Council has been denied by the council itself.

For others the question is a bit more complicated. The church has the right and duty to speak and act in the

---

[36] *The New Delhi Report,* p. 230.

[37] *Ibid.,* pp. 230, 238.

[38] *The Uppsala Report 1968,* p. 291.

[39] *Ibid.,* p. xvii.

[40] For a description of socialist influences in the background of the ecumenical movement see Gaines, *op. cit.,* pp. 30ff.

social sphere, but not every means of doing so is valid. Charles Malik, for instance, has praise for the Commission of the Churches for International Affairs, but says:

> But some of these statements sounded political, in the sense that the churches themselves seemed to lay down a national or international policy. The churches cannot assume responsibility either for the formulation or for the success or failure of such policy. Such responsibility falls squarely on the duly constituted organs of the civil polity. The Church is another society altogether, although it penetrates and judges civil society. The victories and defeats of the Church are not political-international victories and defeats. The Church cannot identify its fate and the name of its Master with the fate of the nations.[41]

We would prefer to locate the criticisms at another point. The concern of Christ, and therefore of His church, is indeed with the whole man. But the church, in expressing that concern, must bear its own character always in mind. This, to be sure, is not foreign to World Council thinking. It is maintained that the church will discover its true character precisely in such activity in the world. But while there is an element of truth in this, it is basically wrong. The identity of the church is not first a subject of empirical inquiry, but a relationship to the God who has spoken. The World Council has not yet succeeded in fighting its way through to a unified understanding of that relationship. If it feels itself ready to launch on a program of activity in the world, it must at least continue to seek the roots of its unity elsewhere at the same time.

Nobody wants an irrelevant theology. What theology is irrelevant? Surely it is one that fails to speak to man's true condition. It is said that there are theologies that view man as a disembodied spirit, floating around in a world without politics, economics, amusements, or sex. If there is such a theology, it surely needs correction. But contemporary activist theology is likewise guilty of failing to speak to man's

---

[41] Charles Malik, "Opportunities for Concern and Action," *ER*, Vol. XIX, No. 2, p. 172. For an extended statement of a similar point of view, see Paul Ramsey, *Who Speaks for the Church?* (1967).

true condition. The fault lies at least in part in an empty and groundless optimism about man. True Christian optimism can take over only after man's weakness in sin has been fully acknowledged and the saving remedy of Jesus Christ applied.

The danger lies not in Christian action, but in an activism that neglects its source and base. If concern with Vietnam, Nigeria, and the race question is all the church is here for, it may well be asked whether the *church* is relevant. Such concern is proper enough, but it is not sufficient to justify the existence or define the character of the church. Even love and peace do not supply that definition. The church exists not only to bring love and peace to the world, but to bring God to the world and the world to God. Without this the love and peace will prove to be little more than a mirage.

Perhaps the question is where the accent is to be laid. Is it not time to be emphasizing the outlook on the world? No; that will take care of itself in our day. The way of the bandwagon is the way of least resistance. A time of shaking of foundations is a time to be looking for those which cannot be shaken. And if ever it was necessary to hold together theory and practice, it is necessary now.

But the far more disturbing question is whether the differences are much more than those of accent. Are the two accents reflections of a totally different way of looking at Christian truth? When one says "sin" and urges redemption, and another says "guilt feelings" and urges psychoanalysis, are they talking the same language? Are those who wish to retain and those who wish to abandon the assembly of a congregation for cultic worship in the same camp? These questions – and a host of them could be framed – run as an unsettling undertone through the various issues we are considering. It would be hard to demonstrate either an affirmative or negative answer to them with finality. But it would be equally hard to deny that they are critically important to the church and to the World Council of Churches.

Varieties of Response: The Church as Mission

With the absorption of the International Missionary Council in 1961 the World Council of Churches became the testing ground for ecumenical missionary theory. This was not as radical a development as might be thought, since the two organizations, while they were still separate, had very close relations with each other. Nevertheless the merger marked an important step, both in the symbolic expression of the doctrine that the church is mission and in the practical effect of church on mission and mission on church. The full impact of this new relationship was seen for the first time at the assembly level at Uppsala.

What emerged at Uppsala in the realm of missions was not due only to that merger seven years earlier. The entire ecumenical movement was strongly under the influence of the great dual challenge which we have described, that of secularity and of the non-Christian religions. What happened in the area of missions at Uppsala may therefore be taken as an indication of the response of the ecumenical church in its mission aspect to that challenge.

Were it not for that new influence from outside, it might have been expected that the broader body – the World Council of Churches – would have gone far to absorb the smaller body – the International Missionary Council. What happened was somewhat the reverse. The World Council was swept along toward a "mission" reaction to the world situation, but in an interpretation of mission hitherto almost unknown in the world.

This is not to suggest that there was a crystal-clear understanding of mission at Uppsala. In fact, it was argued that "there simply is at this time no common understanding of the nature and limitations of the Christian mission or of the method for its implementation."[42] Nor were the theological lines drawn with great clarity. The debate, it is said, "was directed toward what ought to be said and how, rather than

---

[42] *The Uppsala Report 1968*, p. 38.

to the theological issues which underlay the lively disputes on content and wording."[43]

Nevertheless there was a theology that came to expression at Uppsala. The *Drafts for Sections* stated this more unequivocally than the more moderate statement that emerged from the assembly. Consider this eyebrow-raising paragraph:

> We have lifted up humanization as the goal of mission because we believe that more than others it communicates in our period of history the meaning of the messianic goal. In another time the goal of God's redemptive work might best have been described in terms of man turning towards God rather than in terms of God turning towards men.... Today the fundamental question is much more that of *true* man, and the dominant concern of the missionary congregation must therefore be to point to the humanity in Christ as the goal of mission.[44]

Renewal in mission is set in the context of mankind struggling to realize its common humanity.[45] The report approved by the assembly opens with these words:

> We belong to a humanity that cries passionately and articulately for a fully human life. Yet the very humanity of man and of his societies is threatened by a greater variety of destructive forces than ever. And the acutest moral problems all hinge on the question, What is man?[46]

This was the deepest theological note struck in the report. We may say, therefore, that Uppsala's response to the challenge was to see mission in the light of humanization.

There were other mission accents as well, but these played a lesser role. Uppsala built upon the work of the Mexico City missions conference of 1963. Here the scope of missions was seen to include:

> I The witness of Christians to men of other faiths;
> II The witness of Christians to men in the secular world;
> III The witness of the congregation in its neighborhood;
> IV The witness of the Christian Church across national and confessional boundaries.[47]

---

43 *Ibid.*, p. 37.
44 World Council of Churches, *Drafts for Sections* (1968), p. 34.
45 *The Uppsala Report 1968*, p. 36.
46 *Ibid.*, pp. 27f.
47 World Council of Churches, *New Delhi to Uppsala* (1968), p. 25.

With respect to the "witness of Christians to men in the secular world" it was recognized that:

> Rapid urbanization and industrialization create a secular society which progressively affects millions of people in every part of the globe. The fundamental question is therefore, what is the concept and form of mission in an urban-industrial world?[48]

As a practical means to meet the mission challenge, the Division of World Mission and Evangelism proposed "real and effective redeployment of resources in the light of agreed purposes."[49] These decisions, as well as the concrete suggestions made by the Uppsala Assembly, may have immense practical consequences for mission. But their value will depend on the accuracy of the theological insight mentioned above.

Not only will the challenge of secularity and the response in terms of humanization have impact on mission tactics; it will affect the life of the church as well. The delegates to the Conference on Church Union Negotiations in 1967 "were unanimous in the opinion that one of the most important questions they face in negotiations – one which runs through all issues from doctrine to structure – is that of freedom and authority." After reflecting on the erosion of biblical authority, they went on to say: "Finally, with the emphasis increasing on the ministry of the laity, old structures of authority in the Church are challenged because they seem to impede initiative and hamper mission."[50] And the church-which-is-mission is also bound to be affected at the point of asking, "Who is in the church and who is not?"

Some years before Uppsala there was a flurry of discussion of conversion. Making humanization the goal of mission is bound to have some effect on the determination of the answer to this question. The broader concerns in this debate were the issue of conversion as a matter of soul-winning or as a matter of changing human institutions. In an issue of the *Ecumenical Review* devoted to the study of conver-

---

48 *Ibid.,* pp. 30f.
49 *Ibid.,* p. 28.
50 *Midstream,* p. 69.

sion, one author (whose views need not be taken to represent the World Council) argued:

> Groups that can win such radical conversion have, without doubt, their own inner strength and they bring under judgment Laodicean churches that are content to maintain a dwindling conformity without any serious self-criticism. But far from bringing relevant impress and influence upon a secular world, they are in fact in flight from it, and their very capacity for prodigious religious faith rules them out as an option for pure secular men.[51]

It is at this point that we may raise the questions that are suggested by the entire contemporary treatment of missions. If there is any peculiar role for the World Council of Churches in respect to mission, it is to hold together emphases that belong together but tend to diverge. Such, it would appear, are the "radical conversion" and the "relevant impress and influence upon a secular world" that are mentioned above. There is probably little point in mutual recriminations, but it is fair to ask who are most inclined to separate what belongs together. Are those who emphasize individual conversion to Christ more inclined to neglect concern for the world, or is the situation reversed? The above quotation raises, in addition, another question of holding together what should not be separated. If "prodigious religious faith" is not "an option for pure secular men" is the commentator leaving out precisely the heart of the Christian evangel – the renewing work of the risen Christ, through the Holy Spirit whom He has sent?

Our question is whether the newly defined gospel is recognizable in biblical terms. It is not so if it is only a half-gospel, no matter how well that half is portrayed. Is the gospel of a renewed humanity the whole gospel? Or has the trans-cultural process changed the gospel into something radically different? Nontheological emphases, it appears, have been glorified to the detriment of the church and the cause

[51] E. R. Wickham, "Conversion in a Secular Age," *ER,* Vol. XIX, No. 3, p. 295. It should be noted that the same issue of the *Ecumenical Review* also presents biblical word studies on conversion that do little to support Wickham's position.

of Christ. "New humanity" replaces "salvation." This is no improvement.

The voice of dissent is heard within council circles also. Let us listen to two expressions of it:

> Today, too often believers are limited by their own complexes. As in the past too many words were spoken, we are now afraid to speak. As the world has become secularized, we are afraid to pronounce in it the name of its Saviour, preferring a silent presence that easily transforms witness into mere social service. The new theologies about the death of God encourage such an attitude and explain it. Actually they conceal an unconscious desire to be accepted again by the world that we have wearied with our clericalism. But apart from acknowledging our guilt, we must honestly admit that there is no Gospel without the announcement of the Lord's death and resurrection.[52]

Even the Uppsala Assembly refused to be blown completely off its feet by the new emphasis. It would be hard to put the issue more clearly than is done in these words:

> In the section itself the debate was sharper and led to a heated exchange on whether, within the abiding mandate of the Church's mission, concern "for the millions who do not know Christ" still constitutes a decisive imperative. Some would contend that reluctance to speak in these terms is no more than a wish to depart from terminology which no longer communicates what is most desired to express. Others were left wondering whether the differences revealed in this discussion were more fundamental and related to that contemporary "crisis of faith" to which there are various allusions in the following pages and in the light of which one of the contributors to this volume writes, "Perhaps, for the sake of the world, the next Assembly should be more theological."[53]

What the final outcome of this debate will be is not manifest. But if it fails to hold together revelation and experience, the new humanity and the new heart, it will most likely fail also to hold together the churches in the council. The issue that is raised is as basic as all that.

---

[52] Tullio Vinay, "Evangelism and Social Service," *ER*, Vol. XX, No. 2, p. 154.

[53] *The Uppsala Report 1968*, p. xix.

Varieties of Response: Involvement in the World

A third type of response to the new challenge is the contention that the church should be involved in the world. This is a further elaboration of the mission theme, with overtones of activism, secularity, relativity, and possibly revolution. As in the other new developments we have discussed, there is danger that the two sides in this debate shall caricature each other. And again, the question is whether the World Council of Churches can genuinely hold these two sides together. The church is described in appealing terms as being

> not so much a separate sphere — the sacred in contrast to the secular — as the piece of the world that is conscious of Christ's purpose for it.[54]

If that consciousness can be soundly based and clearly maintained, this may prove to be a very fruitful understanding indeed.

Some observers saw the Uppsala Assembly as marking the end of old-style ecumenism, concerned mainly with the internal squabbles of the churches, and a beginning of the world church concerned primarily with the needs of mankind outside the church.[55] Such a new beginning is not absolutely new. A discussion of "responsible society" appeared as early as 1950 in the *Ecumenical Review*,[56] and figured prominently in the work of the Evanston Assembly.[57] Governments and "power structures" must be responsible in the areas of peace, poverty, race, and the like, or be reformed, perhaps even via revolution, to become so. On the inflammatory subject of revolution the council blew neither hot nor cold, but was lukewarm enough to heat certain critics to the boiling point:

> As Christians, we are committed to working for the transforma-

[54] Williams, *op. cit.,* p. 128.

[55] Paul Oesterreicher in *Voyage,* Bulletin of the British Council of Churches, London, 1968.

[56] Wolfgang Schweitzer, "The Bible and the Church's Message to the World," *ER,* Vol. II, No. 2, p. 123.

[57] Cf. Gaines, *op. cit.,* p. 639.

> tion of society. In the past, we have usually done this through quiet efforts at social renewal, working in and through the established institutions according to their rules. Today, a significant number of those who are dedicated to the service of Christ and their neighbor, assume a more radical or revolutionary position. They do not deny the value of tradition nor of social order, but they are searching for a new strategy by which to bring about basic changes in society without too much delay. It is possible that the tension between these two positions will have an important place in the life of the Christian community for some time to come. At the present moment, it is important for us to recognize that this radical position has a solid foundation in Christian tradition and should have its rightful place in the life of the Church and in the ongoing discussion of social responsibility.[58]

One may question the accuracy of the descriptions and the validity of the judgments in that statement. What is beyond question is that the boldness with which the position is advocated and the equanimity with which it was received mark a new beginning in church activity in our time.

But it would be wrong to concentrate on the question of revolution. The new beginning deserves a calmer treatment than that subject is likely to evoke. Colin Williams has summed the matter up well:

> Now that conservative view of the role of the church is under serious challenge. With the breakdown of Christendom, with the revolt of Asia and Africa against the Christian West, and with the challenge of the dispossessed colored to the inherited dominance of the white Christian world, it has become increasingly apparent that the hierarchical views of church and society and the pietist limitations of the church's role to the religious order are hindrances to an understanding of the positive role of the church in the processes of change.[59]

This is revolutionary language, too, but it is revolution of another sort. In words like these one can begin to sense something of what is meant by the plea to make the church relevant to the modern world, and the suggestion that its

---

[58] Report on the World Conference on Church and Society in *ER*, Vol. XIX, No. 1, p. 60.

[59] Williams, *op. cit.*, p. 43.

structures may have to change if that relevance is to be achieved. The conservative churchman may not in justice ask that these concerns be dismissed out of hand. He may only be concerned, as he should, that it be the hindrances, and not the essence, of the church which are abandoned.

We shall not take the time to discuss the wide-ranging subject of new forms of ministry, of pluriform presence in the world,[60] of new programs that the much-maligned suburban parish will have to learn to accept,[61] and the like. Important as these are, we shall be content to sum the matter up by saying that the church is challenged to break out of those structures which cause it to look inward. What is necessary, however, is to indicate that the World Council of Churches is not oblivious to the need of some caution in this area. One of the World Council staff members issued a warning about revolution. Against the background of Nazism he pointed to the great danger of identifying the promises of God or the work of Christ with any particular revolution in the world.[62] In the introduction to the report on World Economic and Social Development at Uppsala, it was pointed out that the church's role was not officially to adopt a political position or undertake the study of technical solutions. The role was much rather to be that of improving understanding and public awareness of the problems.[63] Perhaps the most moving of the testimonies is found in words written by Charles Malik, which might well be taken to apply to the whole round of subjects being discussed in this chapter:

> Some moral and spiritual content must accompany every relationship between the haves and the have-nots. Whatever the relations between the nations, however sordid and hard-headed and based on heartless self-interest they might be, the Church cannot believe in the self-sufficiency of the economic and political. Man and the spirit come first, and the World Council of Churches in interesting itself in the economic and social prob-

60 *Ibid.,* p. 152.
61 Cf. Müller, *op. cit.,* p. 167.
62 H. H. Wolf, *op. cit.,* p. 11.
63 *The Uppsala Report 1968,* p. 41.

> lems of Asia and Africa cannot fail to this point; nor can its member churches fail to urge it on their governments. The newly independent peoples must be disabused of the terrible illusion that all they need is independence and economic development — which is virtually all they hear from their erstwhile masters. How to humanize and spiritualize development should be the principal concern of the churches in this age in which everybody talks and worships development.

And even more to the point, he says, with reference to the "moral crash":

> The end is not moralizing and preaching; the end is not mechanical recipes; the end is "repent and believe the Gospel"; the end is the Holy Ghost falling freely upon the repentant sinner and thoroughly cleansing him.[64]

Will the church remember this as it becomes involved in the world? What, otherwise, is the point of involvement?

Varieties of Response: The Study of Humanity

The one remaining response to consider is the study of Humanity that the council will now undertake. Various studies of this kind are proposed for the next period in the council's life. These include, "Man in Nature and History"; "Humanization"; "Human Institutions in the Mission of God"; and a study on "the anthropological revolution and its implications for Christian theology and the mission of the Church." This is correctly termed "a remarkable convergence of interests on the study of the nature and future of man."[65] This is the theological aspect of the current emphasis. If doctrine is to make any impact on the new shape of the church, it will have to be at this point.

Further light on Theological Anthropology is needed, and there is no denying that it is needed in a special sense today. The crucial questions are whether anthropology is to become the hinge on which everything else turns, what will be the sources of information for the new development, and what will be its relation to other central doctrines? When once

---

[64] Charles Malik, "Opportunities for Concern and Action," *ER,* Vol. XIX, No. 2, pp. 171f.

[65] *The Uppsala Report 1968,* p. 204.

it has been granted that such study is needed, one can hardly go much farther at this point. It is impossible either to endorse or criticize the results of a study before they have come to light. One prediction seems fairly safe. If the conclusions say anything at all, they will not please everybody. But the very predictability of that conclusion stamps it as insignificant. There is not much to do but wait and see.

Just a few questions may be helpful, however. This sudden intense concentration on humanity is a striking phenomenon even before the studies are completed. We are reminded that the World Council's basis was once criticized as concentrating so much on the deity of Christ as to have a heretical flavor.[66] Have the churches of the council now overcompensated for this alleged heresy by talking only of Christ's humanity? Again, we may ask whether the forthcoming studies will succeed in holding together Christian doctrine and contemporary activism. And which of these will lead the other? The intriguing question raised by the sudden convergence of studies on "man" is whether activism has an insight with which theology will catch up only after the fact. If so, will theology baptize the pretheological discovery, correct it, diverge from it, or surrender? Whatever the outcome, theology will be given neither all the credit nor all the blame, for help is on the way:

> . . . in connection with the studies on Man, it becomes essential to supplement theoretical work in the various disciplines with work related to specific human situations. . . . In the past, ecumenical study has largely been carried out by theologically trained people and within a church setting. We believe that in the future the proportion of experts in secular disciplines involved in such study must greatly increase.[67]

Right; let theology get the help it needs where it can be found. But then is it too much to suggest that the theologians

---

[66] William Adams Brown, *Toward a United Church,* p. 146; quoted in Gaines, *op. cit.,* p. 165.

[67] *The Uppsala Report 1968,* p. 204.

be and act like theologians indeed, so that biblical and churchly insights are not lost from view?

The Futility of Theology

We have touched at various points in this chapter on theological questions. We have noted that a whole series of studies in theological anthropology are being projected. Does this refute our contention that theology may be on the way out of existence, at least as far as the World Council is concerned? We do not think so. And if one scratches a bit beneath the surface it appears that the World Council does not think so either. This was evident in the materials prepared for the council's consideration. Of the many quotations that could be adduced from the book, *New Delhi to Uppsala,* we submit just two:

> Another characteristic of the period has been that the theological situation has become more complicated and even confused as new theological tendencies have called in question the results of the theological work of earlier generations. Thus it would seem that in addition to the problem of inter-confessional understanding we now have the additional problem of understanding between theological tendencies within major confessions. This means also that the emerging ecumenical consensus on a number of important points of faith and order or life and work is less stable than had been supposed. . . . In such matters as the authority of the Scriptures and their basic unity or the basis of social ethics we are thrown back to the discussion of our basic assumptions. We have to work out again what the true relation is between the Church and the world and what is the relevance of church unity for the life of the world.[68]

> Finally, the "crisis of faith" is fast becoming the number one problem for the churches as well as for the ecumenical movement. Even the quest for certainty in faith is going out of fashion. Everything is rendered mobile and tentative, including faith itself. What is the Gospel? There is no agreement on the answer to this question. Dare we affirm the kerygma of the death and resurrection of Christ? Or do we confess only a certain "fascination" for an unknown Christ who beckons us towards the unknown future?[69]

---

[68] *From New Delhi to Uppsala,* p. 9.
[69] *Ibid.,* p. 82.

The above quotations should be evidence enough that the World Council is not willingly foisting on the world a problem of its own creation. It is caught up in the sweep of the times. The change from confidence in doctrinal statements to rejection of them came without a formal decision embodying preamble, arguments, and grounds. Nor is modern theology apart from the World Council to blame for all aspects of the situation. There is a conspiracy against Christian theology worthy of a satanic mastermind. As Albert Van den Heuvel has said:

> We have to start all over again in our theological thinking. All sciences have gathered against the Church and its message, and we must confess that our faith may be undaunted but our intellectual understanding of it has taken some severe blows. The historians have taught us that our traditions are less glorious and less factual than we believed. The sociologists have explained to us in how earthly a manner we are organized, the natural scientists do not exactly expect help from us any longer, the language analysts dismiss our pronouncements, and the philosophers call us escapists.[70]

It is important to note also, however, that this situation has its optimistic side. The heart of this optimism lies in the fact that the church's problems arise out of its contact with the world. This is the age in which for the first time Christianity has become a worldwide religion. The accompanying fact, that it is a small minority of the world's population, does not negate this. This is not so much a new fact as a new discovery of a long-existing fact. As such it is a step in the direction of realism. A challenge that arises out of the confrontation of new possibilities, in a spirit of new realism, cannot be all bad. A church that has problems because it is in contact with the world and because it takes the world's problems seriously is more alive than a church that is at ease in Zion. It is improper, we should judge, to distill the whole biblical teaching about the church into a concept of the servant minority and then argue outward

[70] Albert H. Van den Heuvel, "The Honest to God Debate in Ecumenical Perspective," *ER,* Vol. XVI, No. 3, pp. 293f.

from there. But the servant minority is a biblical teaching that is closer to being taken seriously today than it was a generation ago. Even the great new responsibilities laid on the shoulders of the run-of-the-mill layman are an optimistic sign in a way. For these also are not new; they are newly discerned. And the layman with his greater degree of education is better equipped to meet that challenge than in the past — *provided* he is equipped with a clear vision of Christ and His kingdom. There is a potential optimism in this situation; whether the potential can be realized is the burning question of the day.

If the challenge to theology is as overwhelming as it has appeared to be, is it fair to look askance at the World Council for its theological shortcomings? To that question we shall answer no and yes, with the final accent on the yes. Perhaps this look is not so much an accusing as a wistful one. The World Council is in a peculiarly fortunate position, compared with individual denominations. If a successful solution to the contemporary problems were to be found, this would be more likely to be accomplished by the World Council than by any one denomination alone. The council has all the right connections; or at least, if it does not have them, nobody has. In it there is a meeting of East and West, of first, second, and third worlds, of haves and have-nots. Here the theorist and the activist can sit across from each other at the same table. Here is the ability to dip into the pool of auxiliary scholarship to an extent no one denomination can rival. Here mission and church are one.

Why is that ringing theological answer not forthcoming? Part of the answer is the other side of the above coin. The very riches of the council are an embarrassment if it does not have the unity of outlook and interpretation necessary to produce an answer that is not a weak compromise. The council is too rich; it has powers that it is unable to manipulate in a preconceived direction.

But we must not whitewash the council and its theologians too readily. Among the questions we would ask, the first is this: where is the vertebrate theology the church needs?

When Van den Heuvel's array of monsters attacked theology, could the theologians not have been just a bit more stubborn? Or, to put the matter in his terminology, have we "started all over again in our theological thinking" or have we just quit? Kenneth Slack has this rather forlorn commentary on the Uppsala Assembly:

> George Bell of Chichester . . . commented on the Lambeth Conference of 1958 in a letter written in the last days of his life, "Too little of supernatural or spiritual or (if preferred) too little of theological approach anywhere." No one could accuse him of failing in concern for Christian obedience in the world; but he was sure it had to be Christian. Uppsala, too, was not strong in this sense. It did not tackle the crisis for faith.[71]

One casts about for reasons why a church assembly does not come to grips with the crisis of faith. One possible answer is that it has taken the crisis too much into its own bosom. Concern for the natural has led some to pay no more than lip service – and even that grudgingly – to the supernatural. There has been too little of the connection between theology and faith; and now not in the oft-criticized relationship in which theology dictates to faith. What has been lost is a theology that takes faith seriously and operates from it. A faith that has no implications for theology is a peculiar sort of docetism. This is not an accusation that can be leveled at all theologians, to be sure; but that merely raises the further question whether supernaturalists and antisupernaturalists belong in the same organization, seeking to witness to the same faith. Is this not itself a crisis of faith?

Perhaps the World Council would also do well to give some hard thought to the question whether it is not trapped by its own methodology. It has boldly and provocatively attacked various theological themes. But it was been so concerned for catholicity of approach (in the sense of universality) and unity among the member churches that it has left some of these themes hanging in the air. How much clearer the church's path might be if the theme of the Evanston Assembly had been brought to a clear-cut decision!

[71] Slack, *op. cit.,* pp. 87f.

Professors Schlink and Calhoun presented widely diverging papers on the eschatological theme, "Christ – The Hope of the World." Although we have been assured that these two statements were not contradictory,[72] it is certainly also correct that "no common mind can be discerned in the Assembly discussion at this point."[73] But how helpful it would right now if the churches could know what the Bible says about the future toward which they are moving (or the boundaries of their living, if that is the correct meaning of "eschatology").[74]

It is argued, indeed, that the Evanston theme was big enough to include both viewpoints and that most churches were introduced or reintroduced to aspects of eschatology that they had overlooked.[75] But this does not completely absolve the council. It is high time that, rather than merely assert as a matter of course in every doctrinal question, that two opposing views are both parts of the one truth, the council set itself to show *how* apparent contradictions become agreements. In spite of the best of intentions and a galaxy of fine talent, the council is caught up in the ecumenical dictum that everybody has to be right all of the time. Insights thus gained are rather useless for charting a course of action. Small wonder that there are some who think they can sail ahead without the benefit of that kind of help! And a doctrinal discussion full of abstruse terms but devoid of conclusions is also a poor preparation for indoctrination. We recognize that "indoctrination" is as dirty a word for some as "ecumenical" is for others, but they are wrong. If today's layman is to be the church's presence in the world, he needs indoctrination more than the soldier who runs the risk of falling into enemy hands.

Much the same kind of comment could be made about

---

[72] Ralph Douglas Hyslop, "Christ – The Hope of the World," *ER,* Vol. VII, No. 1, p. 21.

[73] *Ibid.*, p. 23.

[74] Robert L. Calhoun, "Christ – The Hope of the World," *ER,* Vol. VII, No. 2, p. 141.

[75] Samuel McCrea Cavert, "Evanston and the American Churches," *ER,* Vol. VII, No. 2, p. 116. See also Hyslop, *op. cit.*, p. 21.

other elements of doctrine, such as the nature of the church's unity. We pass these by, however, to move on to the recognition of a real ecumenical dilemma at this very point. If the World Council gets to the point of saying no to something, instead of attempting the impossible by saying yes to everything, there is going to be a parting of the ways. Catholicity in the extensive sense interferes with catholicity in the sense of adherence to the truth. In other words, the council is faced with the dilemma, not only of holding together various denominations, but of holding that very function together with its function of seeking out the one truth which is the touchstone of the church.

Our concern is that the council shall not resolve this dilemma by giving up its concern for the truth. If the demise of doctrine is to be avoided, it will have to be by conscious effort in such times as these. The council theologians and member churches (and the latter sometimes seem more ready to do this than the former) will have to have the faith that God "our help in ages past" *is* holding the future in His hands. They will have to be as determined to find out what this means as they have been to stay together. This amendment, at least, must be made to the agenda that the world is allowed to write.

And the world must not write the answers. The church that enters the world must be very conscious of its identity. If man is studied, let him be studied in the light of God. Let the council be as ready to say that revolution is not the right way for man to go as it has been to say that war is not. Let the Creator Spirit be traced, but let there be no effort to create Him where He is not, for this is idolatry.

Never has the church's doctrine – however one wishes to name it – been as important to its welfare as it is now. True, the role of doctrine has sometimes been overrated in the past. Or, perhaps more accurately, its connection with the church's activity has been neglected. But this is the wrong time to overcompensate for that particular mistake. There was a time when the church's diaspora situation was thought to be temporary. Missions, it was thought, would overcome this. But:

> It is only now that a passing Christendom realizes that *to be a "diaspora" is the Church's destiny in history* — it is characteristic of the "historicity" of the Church's life.[76]

To recognize this fact is a very healthy thing. But what an utterly wrong time to be neglecting the *esprit,* the knowledge, the tradition of the church! Without any question, the new realization calls for the transcending of some past positions. But this is quite different from repudiating them. And lest the church commit the folly of exchanging them for nothing, it must exchange them for something; and that something has to be clearly understood and clearly stated. If the study of missions produces only dynamics its relation not only to Christian tradition but to Christianity will be questionable. If we do not build on a foundation, the work will not last. If the studies of man produce only a faint and belated echo of theories of man that were conceived without God, it is not only the church that will suffer, but man will be the worse off, too. If that is not a conviction of the church, it might be better to scrap the whole effort.

And now we have come full circle, because the scrapping of the whole theological effort is what some consider a promise and we consider a threat. What makes this intolerable for us is the conviction that the theology which some wish to abandon is a coming-to-expression of faith. Or put the other way around, the faith that the church carries into the world insists on expressing itself — in other ways as well as doctrine, but not least of all in doctrine.

And this is why it is to be fervently hoped that the World Council of Churches will not surrender doctrine to its threatened fate. Action in the world, yes; but let that action be shaped and guided by the teaching of the church, drawn from the Word of God. The doctrine of the church stands today,

---

[76] Wilhelm Dantine, "The Minority Church — An Ecclesiological Survey," *ER,* Vol. XX, No. 1, p. 9.

as always, in need of reformation. But the obsolescence of doctrine is a threat to the very activity that some regard so highly, and a threat to the existence of the church itself.

CHAPTER SIX

SHALL TWO WALK TOGETHER?

THROUGHOUT THIS DISCUSSION THERE HAS BEEN AN UNDER-current of dialogue. The World Council of Churches has been discussed, not from some pinnacle of objectivity, but from a particular point of view. There has been something of an I-thou, or preferably a we-you relationship. It is time now to bring this to a point by considering what the attitude of the one party is to the other party. Although there have been some hints as to this attitude in the preceding pages, these may not have been clear, and they may not have been or seemed to be wholly consistent.

Our summation of this attitude is centered in the biblical query, "Can two walk together except they be agreed?" (Amos 3:3, KJV). It should be quite evident by this time that we are not prepared to give a simple yes or no answer to that question. Our answer must be given only after consideration of three questions that the above question suggests. Who are the two? What is meant by being agreed? And what constitutes walking together?

The first of the two parties of whom we are speaking we shall identify as the World Council of Churches. We need add little to the many things that have been said about this organization on the preceding pages. What is more to the point is that we specify that when we talk about two walking together we mean on the one hand the World Council in the following dimensions: the whole organization, in all of its parts; the council with all of the built-in ambiguities its own proponents recognize; the council as it is *now,* including whatever changes have taken place since the days when its constitution was framed; and the member denominations of that council as well as the council itself. When the second party asks whether it wishes to walk together with the first party, it is this entire entity that it must have in its range of vision.

The problem of identification becomes a great deal more difficult when we ask who the second party is. The "thou" has been identified in all that we have written thus far. But who is the "I"? Perhaps it may seem surprising that any such difficulty exists. Seen from a separate position, no matter how close it may be, the diverse portions of the second party may all appear to be one. But we shall argue that this is not a correct estimate. Perhaps the surprise is shared by some of the "conservative evangelicals" themselves, who think that theirs is a well-defined unity. But they should know better.

The second party that we have in mind is indeed the "conservative evangelicals." We shall be giving some attention presently to the adequacy of that label. These are not the only Christians who are not members of the World Council. The Roman Catholic Church is also not in the council. But this is the only group whose position we shall dare attempt to describe in the present context.

While the conservative evangelical churches may appear as one, and while they may be ready to affirm that they are one in a sense in which the "ecumenical" churches are not, the fact is that in many respects they are not one at all. With respect to church order, doctrine, sacraments, ministry, and the whole gamut of questions involved in the church, there are as many varieties within this group as there are within the World Council — and that despite the fact that the total number of Christians involved is not as large as in the council's membership. Furthermore, those who are lumped together as "conservative evangelicals" include a larger proportion of the small, fragmented, isolated churches than does the World Council. One reason for this, of course, is that a church need not have ten thousand members to join this group, as is the case with the World Council. But there is also something about the "conservative evangelical" group that attracts churches of this sort to it.

There is a unity of a sort among these churches, but it is not easy to identify. As far as concrete issues are concerned, these churches are more united in a negative than in a positive sense. It would not be fair to say that they are "anti-ecumenical." Their attitudes differ widely in this respect. But it is obviously fair to say that they are like each other in respect to the fact that they are not in the World Council. To say that the churches which are not in the World Council are not in the World Council would seem like the height of redundancy except for the fact that this establishes the negative tone of their unity. The negative tone goes just a bit farther than this. All of these churches are theologically right of center, if the center is the World Council. As a consequence, they would probably contend that the World Council is *not* the center, but is left of center.

But even that unity of opposition or negation is not to be overstressed. Although these churches would agree that the council is left of center, they would not all agree as to what puts it in that position. If they were asked what constitutes the center, they would probably give an answer that in some way pointed to Christ, with a very strong emphasis upon His deity, and they would also lay strong emphasis upon the authority and inspiration of the Bible. But if they were asked to explain how this constitutes unity for their party and not for the World Council, which has claimed the same unifying centers, they would all have answers, but their answers would not agree.

Although they agree in opposing the World Council, there are the widest possible differences in the degree of opposition and the manner of expressing it. They would as little like to be judged by each other in this respect as would the churches in the council. Their difference in criticism ranges from those who, after the preaching of the Word, the administration of the sacraments, and the exercise of discipline, make separation from apostasy a fourth mark of the church; to those who make the formal synodical judgment that there is no reason in principle not to join the World Council. Their difference in expression of opposition ranges from the holding of protest rallies to the sending of delegated observers to World Council assemblies, observers who are received with greater courtesy and act with greater circumspection than some of the delegates themselves.

The term "conservative evangelical" is perhaps as adequate as any that could be applied to them, but it leaves a great deal to be desired. It is cumbersome, for one thing; and it would be convenient to have a shorthand term for it. But it is already shorthand for a very diverse group of Christians. This is the real objection. It seeks to say more about the character of these churches than the term can convey.

What the term attempts is to go beyond the "member church" and "non-member church" distinction to say something substantive about the churches thus distinguished. But the problem of defining the terms of the definition remains. What is "conservative" and what is "evangelical"? There are churches, many of them, in the World Council which would be shocked and indignant if these names were denied to them. What, then, is the difference between the "ins" and the "outs"? What is the criterion of judgment as to who merits these names; and who is to apply that criterion?

The fact is that this term is a label and not a definition. We will not attempt to go much beyond this label. To do so might be very profitable for the "conservative evangelicals" and for the rest of the fragments of the church, but it would require probing deeper and discussing longer than we are prepared to do. As to the term "conservative," there is a wide variety of attitudes among these churches as to the manner of conserving the past and the expectations held for the future. As to the term "evangelical," there are great differences as to how wide the gospel is and what its implications are.

Most of what we are prepared to say in elaboration of the member/nonmember distinction may be centered in the term "fundamentalist." We are not, however, proposing this term as a substitute for "conservative evangelical" because of the pejorative meanings with which it has been loaded.

The appropriateness of the "fundamentalist" label consists in a relative difference between the churches of this group and those of the World Council, on such matters of faith as the deity of Christ and the inspiration of the Scriptures. One might add the degree of concentration on preaching the gospel in comparison with the attention paid to social services. The "second party" would be more ready than the "first party" to consider certain aspects of these matters to be essential to the church and to Christian witness. As a consequence, they would also be more ready to decline invitations to fellowship with those who differed with them on these matters. There would even be a tendency to refuse approval to those who, while agreeing with them on these doctrines, differed with them in their evaluation of their importance. In this respect, and in this respect only, the name "fundamentalist" might be applied to them. Any connotations of anti-intellectualism, or opposition to social action *per se,* or of reduction of the Christian position to a short list of "fundamentals" would not be generally applicable to the whole group.

With these explanations, and disclaiming any sufficiency for the term, we may perhaps be permitted for convenience' sake to use the simple term "conservatives." Who speaks for the conservatives thus understood? Nobody does. This is one of the distinguishing characteristics of this group. The Vatican may speak for Roman Catholics, and the Central Committee of the World Council may speak for the member churches of the council, although either point might be contested by some of those who are allegedly spoken for. But there is no semblance of such a centralized voice for the conservatives. As a matter of fact, while some conservatives are seeking a more univocal witness, others appear to be determined that nothing of this sort shall take place.

When we turn to the question what it means to be agreed, we again confront a matter that cannot be settled in a single paragraph. We shall first have to exclude from consideration some criteria that do not and cannot apply to this issue.

The possibility of agreement leading to some kind of co-operation is, first of all, not to be ruled out of the question merely because of the existence, in past or present, of some mutual recriminations. That these exist from the side of the conservatives against the World Council is too well known to require documentation. Perhaps there is less consciousness of a hidden bias from the World Council side against conservatism, but it exists. A few examples must suffice.

In several of the surveys of church union negotiations published in the *Ecumenical Review,* one church is labeled "fundamentalist."[1] This is the only label attached to any of the churches in that country, although there is another one that is as admittedly "liberal" as this one is "fundamentalist." In the *New Delhi Report,* there is a list of five reactions to the new ecclesiastical situation. These are evidently arranged so as to pass from good to bad, since the fifth is "fear." The next to the worst is "conservatism."[2] And in an article in the *Ecumenical Review* one author is so carried away by his eloquence as to say:

> It is unfortunate that there is a debased evangelicalism which remains associated (sometimes through its own fault, sometimes in the popular view) with fundamentalism, conservatism, puritanism, obscurantism, "low church," the drab, the dull, and the deadly.[3]

Not all of these are four-letter words, but in the context they seem to be so intended.

---

[1] Survey of Church Union Negotiations, *ER,* Vol. XII, No. 2, p. 241; *ER,* Vol. XIV, No. 3, p. 363. The reference is to the Presbyterian Churches of Korea.

[2] *The New Delhi Report,* p. 94.

[3] Douglas Webster, "Evangelicalism and the Ecumenical Movement," *ER,* Vol. VI, No. 4, p. 386.

Why should it be only the "fundamentalist" or "conservative" churches that are labeled? An immediate answer to that question is that, in other contexts, "liberal" and "radical" emphases do come in for some negative comment. A less acceptable answer is to argue that the fundamentalist, conservative, and confessional traits are obstacles to ecumenism. We call this less acceptable because it implies that there are no similar obstacles arising from liberalism and anticonfessionalism. But this is a trap into which the World Council should not be willing to fall. For if that is indeed the case, it casts a shadow on the type of ecumenism that is under discussion; it is then something less than truly ecumenical. One might then fairly ask whether the ecumenical position on doctrine and order is really as open as the formal statements indicate. Then the hesitation of the fundamentalist, conservative, or confessional churches in joining the movement can claim some measure of plausibility.

Such instances may be dismissed for our present purpose, however, because they do not reflect the conscious and deliberate attitude of the World Council. The council attitude has been one of consistent openness and invitation. The conservatives were included in the scope of the following four-point decision adopted at New Delhi:

> (1) to reiterate its invitation to churches which accept the basis and purposes of the World Council to apply for membership; (2) to seek contacts with non-member churches with a view to their participation in such activities as may appear to be mutually desirable; (3) to record its pleasure at the presence of the observers of several churches, including the Roman Catholic; and (4) to lay upon the hearts of all member churches the importance of constant prayer for Christian brethren in every part of the world.[4]

In the interim between New Delhi and Uppsala, Eugene Smith published an article in which he listed the things conservative evangelicals have to teach the ecumenical movement.[5] It was reported to the Uppsala Assembly that the

[4] *The New Delhi Report,* p. 42.

[5] Eugene L. Smith, "The Conservative Evangelicals and the World Council of Churches," *ER,* Vol. XV, No. 2.

Division of World Mission and Evangelism had sought to improve relations with conservative evangelicals within both member and nonmember churches. A point mentioned in particular was that observers had been sent to the Wheaton and Berlin conferences on evangelism. The division recognized that its task was only partially carried out, and that further efforts would be needed.[6] The presence of a large number of observers and "delegated observers" from a wide variety of churches was an indication at Uppsala that the attitude of respect and investigation is reciprocated, to some extent, from the other side.[7]

But while the attitude of mutual interest and respect is important, it cannot serve as a criterion for the possibility of further cooperation. It opens up new possibilities of information and understanding. But these of themselves are noncommittal. It is as conceivable that they would lead to further repudiation, the more definite because it was based on closer information, as that they would result in some sort of walking together.

Nor is the criterion to be found in the question whether the conservatives have a right to affirm the council's basis. It would be hard to conceive of one of the conservative churches being challenged on this score. If the basis raised any problems, they would most likely come from the side of the conservatives themselves. These would focus on the question whether the basis was sufficient to support a "fellowship of churches" either in respect to its brevity or in the failure of the council to exercise some sort of discipline in maintaining it.

A more debatable point might be the question whether walking together depends merely on being agreed on the Constitution of the Council and the elaboration of certain points in the Toronto Statement. The problem might be simpler if this were the case. It is evident that both the Constitution and the Toronto Statement have sought to avert some of the dangers that conservatives thought to see

[6] *From New Delhi to Uppsala,* p. 26.
[7] Cf. "List of Participants," in *The Uppsala Report 1968,* pp. 407ff.

in the council in its early years, and even in the years leading up to its First Assembly. But this is, unfortunately, no longer sufficient. The movement has kept on moving. Churches that thus far have not joined no longer have the option of joining the council as it was in 1948 or 1950.[8] All of the past statements have received some measure of interpretation in the council's decisions and actions. The council is not only what the basic documents say it is, but it is what it does.

It is this present character of the World Council of Churches which the nonmember churches have to assess if they are to decide what attitude to take. We shall single out from the issues raised in the previous chapters those which seem to have a particular bearing on the possibilities of agreement between the World Council and the conservative nonmember churches. Only issues of major importance will be considered. The question has never been whether there are any things in the World Council to be criticized. There are such things. A member of the council might accept or reject accusations of a nonmember, but he would find some of his own to make. He would not and need not maintain that the World Council is perfect; and if any criticism assumes that it must be perfect, that criticism itself may be rejected as a complete departure from reality. The question must rather be what issues constitute — rightly or wrongly — substantial barriers to participation of one kind or another.

One of the chief among these is the question of the interpretation of the Scriptures. Only a tiny sample can be given of the many things said about the Scriptures in connection with the World Council of Churches. There never was a time in its history when it was not admitted that the Bible played a crucial role in this movement. The insistence on listening to the Bible in the early years of the council's life

[8] This problem is explored from a Roman Catholic standpoint by Thomas F. Stransky, "Roman Catholic Membership in the World Council of Churches?" *ER*, Vol. XX, No. 3, pp. 205ff. If the Catholic Church joined, he asks, would the World Council have to go back to explorations on the level of comparative ecclesiology?

can hardly be overstated. One article noted how the importance of the scriptural norm increased with the re-examination of the individual confessions:

> For unless the norm of the Word of God, standing above all our seeking and self-questioning, is taken seriously, our quest for the Church in other confessions, and the self-questioning in our own, must end in the dissolution of the Church and in disobedience to the Lord of the Church.[9]

Another made the witness of the Bible the focal point in the churches' contact with each other:

> But since we are concerned with fellowship in Christ, we cannot evade the problem of the Bible. . . . If the occasional utterances and declarations of the World Council of Churches are to be recognized as the witness of Christendom in our day, it must be possible to demonstrate that what is set forth is spoken in obedience to the living Lord of the Church. The most important, indeed many of us would say the only, touchstone is the Bible. The ecumenical movement cannot go beyond the Bible, and the Churches which, in the World Council, have accepted responsibility for one another must constantly challenge one another with the question whether and in what sense the preaching of the Gospel from every individual pulpit can be regarded as the Word of God in our time.[10]

If this were the whole of the story it would be difficult to imagine how conservatives could make an issue of the role of the Bible in the ecumenical movement. It would be practically impossible to find any instance of an ecumenical spokesman flatly contradicting the positions taken in the above quotations. Nevertheless, a problem does exist. It lies in the area of biblical interpretation. Differences on this score have plagued the World Council study committees.[11] The consensus at the Lund Faith and Order Conference went little farther than the agreement that the authority of

---

[9] Edmund Schlink, "The Church and the Churches," *ER,* Vol. I, No. 2, pp. 156f.

[10] Wolfgang Schweitzer, "The Bible and the Church's Message to the World," *ER,* Vol. II, No. 2, pp. 123f.

[11] Cf. Flew, *The Nature of the Church,* pp. 233, 240f.

the Bible is acknowledged.[12] At times it was emphasized that it was a new *critical* Bible theology on which the ecumenical movement should build.[13] That a problem continues to exist with respect to the interpretation, and even the authority of the Bible, was made unmistakably evident by the conference of churches involved in merger negotiations.[14] The Division of Studies finally recognized that the urgency of this question was growing, not decreasing, and authorized a study:

> In view of the importance of the variations in principles of interpretation of the Scriptures characteristic of different church traditions and exemplified by various prominent scholars, the Division invited the Faith and Order secretariat to organize on its behalf a study of biblical hermeneutics. After the important work which has thus far been reviewed by the Faith and Order Commission, it will be necessary to consider how further to take up the questions of biblical authority which are so important for the ecumenical movement as a whole.[15]

It is a courageous act for the council to seek to come to grips with this problem. One may be pardoned for a bit of skepticism as to the ability of a body so ponderous as the World Council to pin down a subject so elusive and erratic as contemporary biblical scholarship. It is also a task of no mean dimensions to avoid the danger on the one hand of producing an official canon of interpretation that might prove seriously deficient in some particulars or on the other hand of saying something so vague that no guidance whatsoever results.

What is the attitude of conservatives to all this? We must distinguish between what they might be urged to do and what they do. One might urge the conservative churches to do any or all of three things: to admit that among them-

[12] Vischer, *A Documentary History of the Faith and Order Movement,* p. 100.

[13] Cf. H. Van der Linde, "The Nature and Significance of the World Council of Churches," *ER,* Vol. III, No. 3, pp. 245f.

[14] "There is the fact that with the earlier ecumenical consensus on biblical authority under question a common ground even for debate seems lacking." *Midstream,* p. 69.

[15] *From New Delhi to Uppsala,* p. 50.

selves there are unsolved problems and unharmonized differences on biblical interpretation; to give thanks that the Bible is being talked about and worked with as much as it is; or to pitch into the ecumenical discussion so that their insights and convictions might be used to benefit others. There are among the conservatives some individuals and groups who are willing to do all three.

But the point to be noted is that the council's attitude toward and difficulties with biblical studies constitute a big obstacle to full participation by evangelicals in the World Council. If there is one doctrinal point at which conservatives are most at one, it is here. Not that they are perfectly agreed on every question of biblical interpretation. But they are one in rejecting any view that so much as threatens to call into question the authority of the Bible. And they consider this important enough to be a criterion for fellowship among Christians. Their criticism of the critical handling of Scripture could hardly be more pointedly stated than has been done by a Roman Catholic observer, when he said about demythologizing:

> This, put at its best, is an attempt to express what the Bible says in language which the ordinary man can understand and which he can feel has a bearing on the conditions of his own life; put at its worst, it looks like a declaration that the Bible is made up of myths, or even fairy stories, to convey the meaning of God's work of Salvation. It may score against a wooden literalism of interpretation and against a failure to realize that words change in meaning and connotation, but it verges upon a denial that there is any final truth, with the implication that all formulations of doctrine become meaningless after a time and may be rejected without loss. This ends in theological pragmatism and leads logically to scepticism.[16]

We shall not attempt to denote or discuss all the possible doctrinal issues between conservative churches and the World Council. The remaining ones which we will discuss will be dealt with quickly, because the issues are similar to those raised by the doctrine of Scripture.

---

[16] Leeming, *The Churches and the Church,* pp. 43f.

A few words must be said about eschatology. One writer has made a particular point of stressing the potential evangelical contribution to the World Council on this doctrine:

> Here again is an undertaking in which the characteristic concern of evangelicals . . . is urgently needed. No new or recovered insights into the meaning for this world of the Incarnation and Atonement must ever be allowed to foreshorten our horizons and to make men indifferent to all those dimensions of our life in Christ into which we shall only enter when the fashion of this world has passed away.[17]

The crucial importance of this doctrine can be seen from two angles. Seen from the side of its derivation, it is a clear instance of the drastic restatement of doctrine that arises out of a critical view of Scripture.[18] The authority of the Bible in the determination of eschatological questions has been seriously undermined:

> It seems obvious to Bultmann, as to most liberal theologians before him, that the historical problem of the New Testament arises from the disappointment of its apocalyptic expectations on the one hand, and from the growing irrelevance to history of the Church's sacramental reinterpretation of those expectations on the other. In a scientific age we cannot understand events in these mythological forms.[19]

The conservatives cannot accept the restatement of eschatology that results from such an attitude as merely a new insight or a new slant on an old doctrine. It looks to them like an abandonment, not only of an old conception, but of an interpretation of eschatology that is consistent with the reliability of the Bible and with the divine nature of Christ. And, looking in another direction, this is a doctrine with the most sweeping implications for the practical life of the churches. The churches must be relevant; agreed.

---

[17] Norman Goodall, "Evangelicalism and the Ecumenical Movement," *ER*, Vol. XV, No. 4, pp. 408ff.

[18] The current doctrinal restatement is connected with a critical view of Scripture and reliance on the theology of experience. Dillenberger and Welch, *Protestant Christianity Interpreted Through Its Development*, p. 203.

[19] Charles C. West, "The Obsolescence of History," *ER*, Vol. XVII, No. 1, p. 5.

But relevant to what? What is the future toward which they must work and for which they must pray? When they say, "Come quickly, Lord Jesus," what do they have in mind? The conservatives find little consolation in the trend of World Council thinking. They may have found the council's performance on the 1954 theme, "Christ – The Hope of the World" painfully indecisive. But they could gain more comfort from the ambiguity of that discussion than from the unambiguous direction of Uppsala's interpretation of the theme, "Behold, I Make All Things New."

We should not leave the impression that all conservatives are agreed in their interpretation of eschatology. It is commonly, but erroneously, thought by distant critics that all conservatives are premillennial in their thinking, just as it is thought by some premillennialists that only they are conservative. Some of the most vigorous battles in the conservative camp have been waged, not only between dispensationalists and nondispensationalists, but between premillennialists and amillennialists. But their differences on what the Bible predicts are nothing compared with the gulf that yawns between them and those who believe that the biblical predictions are inconsequential.

To mention but one more point of doctrine, there is a gulf, conservatives feel, between them and the council on the question of Christology. We shall not repeat what has been said earlier about this crucially important doctrine. Conservatives recognize that there are many within the council who are in basic agreement with them. But they cannot understand how these can profess their solidarity with others who disagree on so absolutely basic a point of faith. It is permissible, they would argue, even commendable, to center all things in Christ. But this lays all the more emphasis on saying a ringing yes to all who believe in the living and resurrected Christ and a resounding no to all who do not.

What view of Christ is it that they repudiate? It would be as hard to indicate that in a few sentences as to define what the true doctrine is. But, with certain slight reservations, H. H. Wolf may be taken to have given a good expression of the conservative position, when he wrote in the *Ecumenical Review:*

> The temptation must be resisted to turn the living person of Christ, "the incarnate God" the revelation of whom is the whole basis of the Bible (although not imprisoned within it) into an *idea* of Christ — a collection of ethical and religious values, nor into a social programme, nor into factors which manifest themselves in new ways during the course of history and which can be traced by the Christian. Then one could revert to these *ideas* as if they were the actual source of Christian preaching and could interpret certain historical forms and events as manifestations of the Christ idea.[20]

Whatever suspicions conservatives may have in this area, they were not likely to be allayed by the emphasis on Christ's humanity that has recently surfaced in ecumenical theology. Whatever toleration the conservatives might learn to exercise, they do not agree that two can walk together without agreement on this point, and they do not aspire to such agreement.

We pass by other doctrinal points for a brief glance at problems of a different order. A word must be said about social activism. It would be inaccurate to say that the conservative churches are opposed to action in the social sphere. These churches in general have been unduly maligned in this respect. Their performance in respect to benevolence was probably not as bad as even their neighbors might think and certainly not as bad as their critics alleged. When we pass from the sphere of individual to corporate action, some of the conservative churches may have an uneasy conscience, but not all need to. At least it can be said that in general there is no denial in principle that the Christian church should engage in social activity for the alleviation of distress among men.

But there are substantial differences between conservatives and the World Council of Churches on the relative importance of this kind of action, the means by which it should

---

[20] H. H. Wolf, "Christ at Work in History," *ER,* Vol. XVIII, No. 1, p. 10.

be carried out, its relation to the preaching of the gospel of salvation, and the tone and tenor of the activity itself. We will not attempt to pass judgment on the validity of all these positions, but must state as a matter of fact that conservatives are strongly inclined to think that it is not the business of the church to make pronouncements in the sphere of politics or economics; that the gospel of redemption from sin through Christ's blood is the basic consideration, to which social activity is an adjunct; that the World Council attitude to social problems tends to be strongly leftist; and that this whole round of activity plays much too large a role in council activities. Those among the conservatives who have been emphasizing that the council is a place for churches to meet one another and witness to each other concerning the gospel have had their argument rendered much more difficult by such recent events as the 1966 Conference on Church and Society and the Uppsala Assembly with its activist orientation. It is hard to imagine any one of the conservative churches agreeing that revolution as a means of change has a legitimate place in the church's program and an honored place in its history. (They would be properly shocked at the suggestion that Luther's revolution had anything in common with the revolutionary ferment observable today. They might, however, be inconsistent enough not to repudiate the iconoclasm of the early Reformation period. Such inconsistency would be matched by that of their opponents in reversing both of those judgments.) The tolerance of revolution, it is thought by its advocates, is a step toward reconciliation. This is hard to believe. But however that may be, it is a step toward alienation of the conservative churches. It is probably not to the credit of these churches that the political and economic issues loom as large as they do. This is, in its way, a suggestion that they lay as much emphasis as council members do on social questions, but stand on the other side of the question of direction. But we are trying to state facts, and the fact is that there is a degree of estrangement here which makes the question of full participation difficult for some and impossible for others.

And finally a word may be said about mission, a subject that is dear to the hearts of many of the conservative churches. They are very deeply concerned that the ecumenical attitude to mission is swinging much too far in the direction of radical theology. At heart their concern in the area of mission is the same as in other areas. Is the gospel being lost in the contemporary enthusiasm for relevance? Conservatives are concerned to ask not only "relevance *to* what?" but "relevance *of* what?" They note with appreciation that World Council member churches wish to accord the younger churches full maturity as soon as possible. But they note also that strong pressures are put on those younger churches which show less than complete enthusiasm for the ecumenical movement. They note with concern the decline in mission staff among churches that are members of the council, a decline that has not affected the conservative nonmember churches. They are convinced that the council's mission effort, whatever the profitable mission insights it has produced, has gone off course toward either unity or social activism or both. They are determined not to participate in a joint "redeployment of forces" with such parties lest they fail in their duty to Christ whose mission it is.

To sum up the disagreements, they have come to center in the relationship of the council with radical theology. This is not essentially different from the earlier situation, in which it was the liberalism of the council that was attacked. The conservatives have been concerned from the beginning that the council represented a type of theology with which they were in fundamental disagreement. The development of radical theology has not changed that attitude, except to accentuate it. What has changed, among some at least, is that it has come to be recognized that there is a conservative as well as a radical accent within the council. But this does not solve their problem. They are upset by the inability of the council to withstand the radical emphasis, or even to face up to it squarely. They are frankly afraid of the price that a more conservative emphasis may have to pay by accommodation to it. To the argument that the radical emphasis is in the world anyway, and the council is the place for a convinced conservative to meet it head-on, they are inclined to say that a conservative church has already so compromised its witness by joining that it will no longer be able to withstand the radical emphasis as it should.

This situation is not drastically improved by the mutual recognition that conservatives are not uninterested in the world and radicals are not uninterested in the Bible. The gulf that remains over the question which should interpret which still appears unbridgeable to many. There is a sharp difference also in respect to the Christian hope. The conservatives are quite certain that a realistic assessment of man makes it absolutely necessary to take into account human depravity. They are in their way more realistic here than the radical theologians. But they are not more pessimistic. They are convinced of the power of the risen Christ to overcome the effects of this depravity as in His death He has already assumed its punishment. And between them and those who use the same terms with a radically different meaning there is, they are convinced, a gap that will have to be bridged before there is any unity about which or within which to witness to the world.

What about walking together, then? It is not getting any easier. Earlier doubts have been removed and earlier misconceptions clarified. But new problems are arising. The conservatives do not find these problems alleviated by bland compromise statements. Rather they find them complicated by the bold public utterances of the council.

Against this background, walking together is difficult. Not all aspects of it present equal problems. Does walking together mean doctrinal discussion? This might be the easiest aspect of it for the conservatives to pursue. But they would have to recognize that, in view of their reservations, they would have to enter upon these conversations militantly, determined to strengthen the conservative wing of the council.

Does walking together mean joint action? This is more

of a problem. It is particularly in this area that membership of conservatives is growing more difficult, not less. Their insistence on doctrinal agreement and on the essential character of some of the doctrines on which there is disagreement makes cooperation in social activities a problem. This becomes even more apparent when the distinction between social and benevolent action and mission witness is being blurred. The former might seem to require a minimum of doctrinal unity; the latter requires basic agreement. If mission witness turns into social activity, the latter comes to require all the agreement in doctrine that is implied in the preaching of the gospel. Joint action in mission is very difficult without that measure of agreement which is implied in the terms "conservative" and "evangelical." To be frank, the conservative evangelicals are not very adept at mission cooperation even among themselves. Joining forces in a common witness with all of the member churches of the council would be for them well-nigh an impossibility.

Does walking together mean *koinonia?* This is the most difficult of all. Despite disclaimers of a deep significance in this word, it carries profound implications. It professes a oneness in Christ that certainly goes far beyond the recognition of the vestiges of the church in some other groups of people. It requires much more than an unregulated and unsupervised adherence to the council's basis. If it seeks to appeal to conservatives, the council is caught here by its own ambiguity. In order to bring churches together it professes to require only a minimum of recognition of one another. But from the outset it claims for that group which has come together a fellowship expressive of the deepest and tenderest relationship of those who are one in Christ. A conservative church, taking seriously what the church says about itself, would have to close both eyes to some inconsistencies in order to join. Thus far the nonmember conservatives have not been willing to wink even one eye at them.

Some would consider the above remarks to be entirely too concessive to the World Council of Churches. Others would take them to express a conservatism that is determined to be isolationist. The two would find it hard to understand each other's attitudes. But we have attempted to be as factual as possible in the above description. We have, to be sure, departed from a purely detached standpoint at times. But we shall have to depart farther now, in order to make some positive suggestions as to what ought to be done at this point.

If it should be concluded that conservatives cannot take up membership in the World Council of Churches, several questions remain. In fact, the more important questions remain, because the World Council is nothing more than a means to an end. Membership or nonmembership in the council is incidental to more basic concerns. The questions are these: Have the conservative churches, by a negative answer to the question of council membership, discharged their responsibility to their fellow Christians? If membership is not possible now, will it be possible at some other time and under some other conditions? If full membership is not possible, is any relationship other than sheer negativism to be considered? Perhaps the questions can be summed up in this one: Have the conservative churches done justice to the cause of Christ and of His church by simply saying no?

It is highly important to a profitable discussion that the question of World Council membership be taken out of the area of anathema. The simple fact is that there are some churches that are members of the council, but differ from some of the nonmember conservative churches only in that one respect. They have an equal love for Christ and the Bible, an equal distaste for radical restructuring, and even a similar dislike for some council actions and utterances. But they are convinced that their place is in the council. This is a question of attitude and strategy, not of faith or nonfaith. Such member churches are not necessarily, or even probably, expressing a waning commitment to their positions by joining. They may be so sure of their position and its value for others that joining the council becomes the thing they absolutely must do. They are as little to be condemned as are the nonmember churches; the member churches do not necessarily have an insufficient commitment to the gospel, and the nonmember churches do not necessarily have an insufficient love for their brethren. Mutual recriminations are not called for.

What is necessary is that the conservative churches consider what is their ecumenical calling. We shall not attempt to repeat or summarize all the excellent things that have been said and written about the unity which, according to the Bible, is both God's gift and His demand. Nor shall we reflect on the growing consciousness that Christianity, no matter how broadly defined, is a dwindling minority in this world and badly needs whatever true unity it can find. But in passing these things by we are not indicating that we consider them untrue or unimportant. We are only building on the fact that they have been argued so eloquently, so fully, and so convincingly, that they need no repetition. Anyone who is unfamiliar with these arguments has only himself to blame, and anyone who is unconvinced by them will not be convinced by the addition of a few words here.

There are, however, two considerations that we would add, partly because they are new and partly because they arise out of the other chapters in this book. The first is the growing consciousness that Christians need each other in order to face the problem of interpreting our age. There is, indeed, a physical need in the world to which Christian action ought to be addressed. But greater and more basic is the need of understanding the world as we now "know" it. There are great opportunities and perils for the church in our day. The opportunity to let God's revelation shine with a clearer light is present. So is the peril of trying to understand the world without that revelation. Conservatives are much concerned that we shall not abandon revelation, and they are right; because if that should happen, the world would not be truly understood and the church would cease to exist. They are concerned to maintain that divine judgment and human sin are necessary ingredients for understanding, and that the way of salvation is still and will always be that of redemption through the blood of Christ. But love and humility must move them to seek contact with other Christians; the love that moves them to share their cherished insights with other men, and the humility that admits that the understanding of this world has gotten a bit beyond us, and we need help and cooperation in regaining it. Talking to themselves will not produce this for the conservatives. They need precisely the challenge of those who disagree with them.

The other consideration is the counterpart of a warning we have issued to the World Council of Churches. It is proper, we think, to warn the ecumenical movement not to institutionalize unity before the unity can bear the weight of an institution. But it is equally in place to warn the conservatives not to institutionalize disunity until it is clear beyond all doubt that the two parties are not one. A careful consideration of the matter must lead to the conclusion that, however important a discrimination between truth and error may be, membership or nonmembership in the World Council is not the proper place at which to draw that line of demarcation. It will be a sad day for the whole Christian witness, their own included, when the conservative churches identify faithfulness with nonmembership and apostasy with membership in the council. Even if at some future time the council should merit such a condemnation, which it does not now, that would be to confuse the issues. Faithfulness to Christ certainly suffers from lack of clear expression if it is submerged in the institutionalization of an anticonciliar attitude. And short of that sad day — may it never come — when council membership becomes the mark of apostasy, conservatives must be careful not to rush in where angels fear to tread. To rush to recognize a disunity that Christ does not recognize is to fail to discern Christ Himself. For the conservative as for any other Christian, this is the ultimate failure of all.

Shall two walk together, then? In spite of all appearances, the two *are* walking together. They have at least a semblance of mutual concern for the cause of Christ and mutual concern for the world. Not only do the churches lack the right, they lack the ability to ignore the ecumenical movement. The question is not whether to participate, but what form of participation each is to adopt. These can range all the way from full participation to unmitigated criticism. The former is at present an impossibility for some conservative churches. The latter is inconsistent with the seriousness of their commitment to the cause of Christ.

One might facetiously suggest that the solution is to assert that there is a spiritual unity between member and nonmember churches, that each recognizes the vestiges of the church in the other, and that they can let the matter go at that. The trouble with that suggestion is that the first part of it is so true. There is a spiritual unity; where it is, what it consists of, and how much of it there is may not be clear. But something of it is there. But if it is there, it cannot be left at that point. It must come to some sort of expression.

The form of expression that seems most open to conservative churches at present is that of maintaining contact with the World Council of Churches short of full membership. They may take seriously the desire of the New Delhi Assembly to "seek contacts with non-member churches with a view to their participation in such activities as may appear to be mutually desirable."[21] Some form of dialogue, especially on the level of Faith and Order conferences, should be possible. The only reason not to allow these contacts, it would appear, would be a lack of confidence on the part of the conservatives; or we might add, a lack of concern. They might fail in confidence that their position would stand up under scrutiny, or they might fail in concern to win others for it. Either possibility would and should be instantly repudiated by any conservative worthy of the name.

Dialogue does, of course, imply that there is something churchly to address. If the approach is to be a mission to heathen rather than a dialogue with churches it ought to be frankly understood by all parties as such. But we are advocating nothing of that kind. Dialogue implies a tacit

---

[21] *The New Delhi Report,* p. 42.

acceptance of the ground rules laid down in the Toronto Statement. If this should seem too high a price to pay, it must be remembered that this provides a freedom to address the World Council without muffling one's witness or becoming responsible for actions the World Council takes in other areas than that of doctrinal confrontation and discussion. Churches that participate as full members of the council are theoretically free to make drastic criticisms of the council's doctrinal deliverances. However that may prove to be in actual fact, churches that participate only in that discussion, apart from full membership, are even more at liberty. They are quite free to criticize the results of a discussion. And they can do so the more intelligently, sympathetically, and effectively if they have actually participated in the discussion. And let it be remembered also that Christian churches do have a responsibility for each other. This responsibility does not cease when another church departs from the truth in some respect. In fact, this increases the responsibility. But under present circumstances, the only place where contact, with a view to witness, can be made with some other churches is in the World Council or the activities related to it.

If this avenue is to be pursued wisely and to the glory of Christ, it requires better knowledge of the World Council by conservative churches. Better knowledge requires closer attention. Closer attention requires increased contacts. Appointment of observers to assemblies, nonhysterical articles in the local church press, well-planned information sessions through theological schools and other agencies are required.

But something else is required also. The conservatives must learn to speak with a unified voice much better than they have done in the past. If every nonmember church should address the World Council at the same time, the cacophony of voices would be unintelligible and unendurable. The conservatives have a great deal to learn in this respect. To seek to speak with a unified voice might give them more of an appreciation of the dimensions of the problem the World Council faces in seeking the very same thing. It would also serve to clarify for the conservatives the nature and bounds of that unity which they claim to have among themselves and which they do not have with the World Council of Churches. It would give them much-needed experience and practice in speaking intelligibly to others and listening attentively as well. The practice gained in achieving joint utterance with those of the same theological camp would be invaluable preparation for their speaking and listening to the World Council and its member churches. And it would, for that matter, be preparation for speaking to the world and listening to it, both in the name and for the sake of Christ.

Whether or not the doctrine of the church has passed its pretheological phase, it certainly is past its pre-ecumenical phase. This is a time for speaking the truth in love, without softening the accent on either. It is, as always, a time for unreserved commitment and plain speaking. But it is also, as always, a time for mutual respect and judgments of charity. "By this shall all men know that ye are my disciples."

BIBLIOGRAPHY

Books and articles relating to the ecumenical movement are so numerous that the construction of an exhaustive bibliography is well-nigh impossible. This bibliography will be restricted to the works consulted in the production of this book. For further bibliographical suggestions the reader is referred especially to Crow, *The Ecumenical Movement in Bibliographical Outline,* National Council of Churches, New York, 1965, 80 pp. Several of the works listed below also have extensive bibliographies.

GENERAL HISTORIES

Rouse, Ruth, and Neill, Stephen (eds.), *A History of the Ecumenical Movement,* Westminster, Philadelphia, 1954, 822 pp.
A standard work, tracing ecumenical concern throughout history and concentrating on the modern ecumenical movement through the formation of the World Council of Churches.

Gaines, David P., *The World Council of Churches: A Study of Its Background and History,* William L. Bauhan, Peterborough, N. H., 1966, 1302 pp.
A full account of the World Council and its constituent organizations, containing much documentary material and a good bibliography.

COUNCIL-RELATED PUBLICATIONS

Ehrenstrom, Nils, and Muelder, Walter (eds.), *Institutionalism and Church Unity,* Association Press, N. Y., 1963, 378 pp.

Flew, R. Newton (ed.), *The Nature of the Church,* Harper, N. Y., 1952, 347 pp.

Goodall, Norman (ed.), *The Uppsala Report 1968,* WCC, Geneva, 1968, 513 pp.
The official report of the Fourth Assembly of the World Council.

Minear, Paul S. (ed.), *Faith and Order Findings,* Augsburg, Minneapolis, 1963.
Preparatory studies for the Montreal Conference.

———, *The Nature of the Unity We Seek,* Bethany, St. Louis, 1958, 304 pp.

———, *The Old and the New in the Church,* Augsburg, Minneapolis, 1961, 96 pp.

Rodger, Patrick, and Vischer, Lukas (eds.), *The Fourth World Conference on Faith and Order,* Association Press, New York, 1964, 127 pp.

Skoglund, John E., and Nelson, J. Robert, *Fifty Years of Faith and Order,* Bethany, St. Louis, 1964, 159 pp.
A helpful summary and interpretation of Faith and Order activities.

Tomkins, Oliver (ed.), *The Third World Conference on Faith and Order,* SCM Press, London, 1953, 380 pp.

Vischer, Lukas (ed.), *A Documentary History of the Faith and Order Movement,* Bethany, St. Louis, 1963, 246 pp.
A judicious selection of documents relating to Faith and Order, providing a handy reference volume.

Visser 't Hooft, W. A. (ed.), *Man's Disorder and God's Design,* Harper, New York, 1949.
The report of the Amsterdam Assembly.

———, *The Evanston Report,* Harper, New York, 1955, 360 pp.

———, *The New Delhi Report,* Association Press, New York, 1962, 443 pp.

WCC, *The First Six Years,* Geneva, 1954, 149 pp.

WCC, *Evanston to New Delhi,* Geneva, 1961, 288 pp.

WCC, *New Delhi to Uppsala,* Geneva, 1968, 220 pp.
The above three books are accounts of the work of the Central Committee during the periods indicated.

WCC, *Work Book for the Assembly Committees,* Geneva, 1968, 200 pp.

WCC, *Drafts for Sections,* Geneva, 1968, 136 pp.

RELATED WORKS

Aubert, Roger (ed.), *Progress and Decline in the History of Church Renewal,* Concilium, Vol. 27, Paulist Press, New York, 1967, 183 pp.
The historical context of the ecumenical movement from a Roman Catholic viewpoint.

Braaten, Carl E., *History and Hermeneutics,* Westminster, Philadelphia, 1966, 205 pp.
Indicates the theological context of ecumenical studies.

Brown, William Adams, *Toward a United Church,* Scribner's, New York, 1946, 264 pp.

Brunner, Emil, *Dogmatics*: Vol. III, *The Christian Doctrine of the Church, Faith, and the Consummation,* Lutterworth, London, 1962, 457 pp.

Dillenberger, J., and Welch, Claude, *Protestant Christianity Inter-*

preted Through Its Development, Scribner's, New York, 1954, 340 pp.

Dillistone, F. W., *The Structure of the Divine Society,* Westminster, Philadelphia, 1951, 263 pp.

Ehrlich, Rudolf J., *Rome, Opponent or Partner?,* Westminster, Philadelphia, 1966, 295 pp.
A searching Protestant inquiry into theological differences between Protestantism and Roman Catholicism.

Harvey, Van Austin, *The Historian and the Believer,* Macmillan, New York, 1966, 301 pp.

Küng, Hans, *The Structures of the Church,* Nelson, New York, 1964, 358 pp.

Leeming, Bernard, *The Churches and the Church,* Newman, Westminster, Md., 1960, 364 pp.
A well-informed critical survey of Protestant ecumenism by a Roman Catholic.

Lowell, C. Stanley, *The Ecumenical Mirage,* Baker, Grand Rapids, 1967, 205 pp.
A sharp attack on the ecumenical movement.

Mackay, John A., *Ecumenics, the Science of the Church Universal,* Prentice-Hall, Englewood Cliffs, N.J., 1964, 294 pp.
A theology of the ecumenical movement with special emphasis on the missionary origins and potential of the movement.

Mascall, E. L., *The Recovery of Unity,* Longmans, Green, London, 1958, 242 pp.

———, *The Secularization of Christianity,* Darton, Longman, & Todd, London, 1965, 286 pp.
Incisive critiques of modern trends from a high Anglican viewpoint.

Neill, Stephen C., *The Church and Christian Union,* Oxford University Press, 1968, 423 pp.
A series of penetrating lectures based on wide knowledge.

Rahner, Karl, *Studies in Modern Theology,* Herder, Freiburg, 1965, 462 pp.

Robinson, James M., *The New Hermeneutic,* Harper and Row, New York, 1964, 243 pp.

Schlink, Edmund, *The Coming Christ and the Coming Church,* Oliver and Boyd, Edinburgh, 1967, 333 pp.

Slack, Kenneth, *Uppsala Report,* SCM Press, London, 1968, 88 pp.
An illuminating day-by-day diary of the Uppsala Assembly.

Visser 't Hooft, W. A., *No Other Name,* SCM Press, London, 1963, 128 pp.
A study of the finality of Jesus Christ with helpful interpretations of the progress of the ecumenical movement.

Welch, Claude, *The Reality of the Church,* Scribner's, New York, 1958, 254 pp.

Williams, Colin W., *The Church* (Vol. IV in the series, *New Directions in Theology Today*), Westminster, Philadelphia, 1968, 187 pp.
Especially helpful for discerning the trends within the ecumenical movement.

Willis, J. J., *et al., Towards a United Church, 1913-1947,* Edinburgh House Press, 1947, 206 pp.
Concerned mainly with the emergence of the Church in South India, but illuminating the problem of a united ministry.

ARTICLES IN THE *ECUMENICAL REVIEW*

Afanassieff, N., "The Ministry of the Laity in the Church," Vol. X, No. 2.

Alivisatos, Hamilcar, "Orthodoxy, Protestantism, and the World Council of Churches," Vol. VI, No. 3.

———, "The Proposed Ecumenical Council and Reunion," Vol. XII, No. 1.

Bainton, Roland, review of *A History of the Ecumenical Movement,* Vol. IV, No. 4.

Berdyaev, Nicholas, "The Unity of Christendom in the Strife Between East and West," Vol. I, No. 1.

Best, Ernest, "The Body of Christ," Vol. IX, No. 2.

Boer, Harry, "The Glory of Christ and the Unity of the Church," Vol. XII, No. 1.

Bridston, Keith, "The Future of Faith and Order," Vol. XI, No. 3.

Brilioth, Yngve, "A New Beginning," Vol. I, No. 1.

Brunner, Peter, "The Realism of the Holy Spirit," Vol. III, No. 3.

Calhoun, Robert L., "Christ – The Hope of the World," Vol. VII, No. 2.

Cassian, Bishop, "The Family of God," Vol. IX, No. 2.

Cavert, Samuel McCrea, "Evanston and the American Churches," Vol. VII, No. 2.

Chirgwin, A. M., "Have the Bible and Its Circulation Any Significance for the Ecumenical Movement?" Vol. VI, No. 3.

Clark, Elmer T., "Non-Theological Factors in Religious Diversity," Vol. III, No. 4.

Craig, A. C., "A Scottish Reflection on Lund," Vol. V, No. 2.

Craig, Clarence T., "The Reality of the Church and Our Doctrines About the Church," Vol. III, No. 3.

Cullmann, Oscar, *et al.,* "Comments on the Decree on Ecumenism," Vol. XVII, No. 2.

Dahl, N. A., "The People of God," Vol. IX, No. 2.

Dantine, Wilhelm, "The Minority Church – An Ecclesiological Survey," Vol. XX, No. 1.

Devanandan, Paul David, "The Christian Message in Relation to the Cultural Heritage of India," Vol. II, No. 3.
Dietzfelbinger, Wolfgang, "Vestigia Ecclesiae," Vol. XV, No. 4.
Douglass, H. Paul, "Some American Reactions to Amsterdam," Vol. I, No. 3.
Dun, Angus, "We Intend to Stay Together," Vol. II, No. 3.
d'Espine, Henri, "The Apostolic Succession as an Ecumenical Issue," Vol. IV, No. 2.
———, "The Role of the World Council of Churches in Regard to Unity," Vol. XIII, No. 1.
Evdokimov, Paul, "The Evangelistic Situation," Vol. II, No. 1.
Goodall, Norman, "Evangelicalism and the Ecumenical Movement," Vol. XV, No. 4.
Gray, Francis, "The Apostolic Succession as an Ecumenical Issue," Vol. IV, No. 2.
Hardy, E. R., "The Bounds and Pillars of the Church," Vol. XII, No. 2.
Hayward, Victor E., "The World Council's Fourth Assembly," Vol. XIX, No. 1.
Hebert, Gabriel, "The Church Which Is His Body," Vol. IX, No. 2.
Hodgson, Leonard, "Faith and Order's Vision of Unity," Vol. XII, No. 3.
Horton, Douglas, "Episcopal and Non-Episcopal Ministries," Vol. VIII, No. 3.
Horton, Walter M., "Continuity and Reform," Vol. I, No. 4.
Iakovos, Archbishop, "The True Nature of the World Council — A Personal Understanding," Vol. XIII, No. 4.
Jenkins, Daniel, "The Ecumenical Movement and Its 'Non-Theological Factors,'" Vol. III, No. 4.
Jung, Eva-Marie, "Roman Catholic Impressions of the Evanston Assembly," Vol. VII, No. 2.
Keller, Adolf, "Stockholm 1925 in the Light of 1950," Vol. II, No. 4.
Kinder, Ernst, "Protestant-Roman Catholic Encounter as Ecumenical Obligation," Vol. VII, No. 4.
Knox, R. Buick, "Archbishop Ussher and Richard Baxter," Vol. XII, No. 1.
Kotzé, J. C. G., "The Meaning of Our Unity in Christ," Vol. VII, No. 4.
Machovec, Milan, "Evangelism and Missionary Activity from a Marxist Viewpoint," Vol. XX, No. 1.
Malik, Charles, "Opportunities for Concern and Action," Vol. XIX, No. 2.
Maury, Pierre, "Evangelism — The Mission of the Church to Those Outside Her Life," Vol. VII, No. 1.
Mehl, Roger, "The Ecclesiological Significance of the World Coun-

cil of Churches from a Roman Catholic Standpoint," Vol. IX, No. 3.
———, "The Ecumenical Situation," Vol. XVI, No. 3.
———, *et al.,* "Some Critical Observations," Vol. XIV, No. 2.
Morrison, Charles Clayton, "The Ecumenical Trend in American Protestantism," Vol. III, No. 1.
Mudge, Lewis S., "World Confessionalism and Ecumenical Strategy," Vol. XI, No. 4.
———, "The Holy Communion at Ecumenical Meetings," Vol. XIII, No. 3.
Müller, Eberhard, "The Structure of Modern Society and the Structure of the Church," Vol. XI, No. 2.
Nelson, J. Robert, "Many Images of One Church," Vol. IX, No. 2.
Newbigin, Lesslie, "One Body, One Gospel, One World," Vol. XI, No. 2.
Nicholls, William, "The Ecumenical Movement and the Doctrine of the Church," Vol. IV, No. 1.
Niles, D. T., "Our Search for Unity," Vol. III, No. 4.
Nissiotis, N. A., "The Ecclesiological Significance of Inter-Church Diakonia," Vol. XIII, No. 2.
Outler, Albert C., "From Disputation to Dialogue," Vol. XVI, No. 1.
Payne, Ernest A., "Working Out the New Delhi Statement on Unity," Vol. XIV, No. 3.
Persson, Per Erik, "The Two Ways – Reflections on the Problem of the Ministry," Vol. XVII, No. 3.
Prenter, Regin, "Catholic and Evangelical," Vol. I, No. 4.
Ramsey, A. M., "Amsterdam and the Doctrine of the Church," Vol. I, No. 4.
Schlink, Edmund, "The Church and the Churches," Vol. I, No. 2.
———, "Changes in Protestant Thinking About the Eastern Church," Vol. X, No. 4.
———, "The Significance of the Eastern and Western Traditions for the Christian Church," Vol. XII, No. 2.
———, "Worship in the Light of Ecumenical Theology," Vol. XIII, No. 2.
Schneider, Carl Edward, "Ecumenical Reformation," Vol. V, No. 2.
Schweitzer, Wolfgang, "The Bible and the Church's Message to the World," Vol. II, No. 2.
Schweizer, Eduard, "The Local Church and the Universal Church," Vol. VIII, No. 3.
Shaull, Richard, "The Christian World Mission in a Technological Era," Vol. XVII, No. 3.
Sittler, Joseph, "The Shape of the Church's Response in Worship," Vol. X, No. 2.
———, "Called to Unity," Vol. XIV, No. 2.

Smith, Eugene, "The Conservative Evangelicals and the World Council of Churches," Vol. XV, No. 2.
Soucek, J. B., "The Good Shepherd and His Flock," Vol. IX, No. 2.
Stählin, Wilhelm, "Insights and Open Questions Concerning Ways of Worship," Vol. IV, No. 3.
Stewart, H. L., "The Present Opportunity of the Church," Vol. II, No. 4.
Stirnimann, Heinrich, "'Catholic' and 'Evangelical,'" Vol. XVIII, No. 3.
Stransky, Thomas F., "Roman Catholic Membership in the World Council of Churches?" Vol. XX, No. 3.
Thomas, M. M., "The Churches in the Political Struggles of Our Day," Vol. III, No. 2.
Thurian, Max, "The Visible Unity of Christians," Vol. XIII, No. 3.
Tomkins, Oliver, "The Church, The Churches, and the Council," Vol. IV, No. 3.
———, "Implications of the Ecumenical Movement," Vol. V, No. 1.
———, "Legitimate Hopes and Legitimate Fears About the World Council of Churches' Role in Churchly Unity," Vol. XII, No. 3.
Torrance, Thomas F., "What Is the Church?" Vol. XI, No. 1.
Vajta, Vilmos, "Confessional Loyalty and Ecumenicity," Vol. XV, No. 1.
Van den Heuvel, Albert H., "The Honest to God Debate in Ecumenical Perspective," Vol. XVI, No. 3.
Van der Linde, H., "The Nature and Significance of the World Council of Churches," Vol. III, No. 3.
Van Dusen, H. P., "The Significance of Conciliar Ecumenicity," Vol. XII, No. 3.
Verghese, Paul, "Will Dialogue Do?" Vol. XVIII, No. 1.
Vinay, Tullio, "Evangelism and Social Service," Vol. XX, No. 2.
Vischer, Lukas, *et al.*, "The Meaning of Catholicity," Vol. XVI, No. 1.
Vischer, Lukas, "The World Council of Churches – Fellowship of All Churches," Vol. XX, No. 3.
Visser 't Hooft, W. A., "The Roman Catholic Church and the First Assembly of the World Council of Churches," Vol. I, No. 2.
———, "Our Ecumenical Task in the Light of History," Vol. VII, No. 4.
———, "Various Meanings of Unity and the Unity Which the World Council of Churches Seeks to Promote," Vol. VIII, No. 1.
———, "Notes on Roman Catholic Writings Concerning Ecumenism," Vol. VIII, No. 2.
———, "The Super-Church and the Ecumenical Movement," Vol. X, No. 4.
———, "The Una Sancta and the Local Church," Vol. XIII, No. 1.

———, "Pluralism—Temptation or Opportunity?" Vol. XVIII, No. 2.
Weber, Hans-Reudi, "The Laity in the Apostolic Church," Vol. X, No. 3.
Webster, Douglas, "Evangelicalism and the Ecumenical Movement," Vol. VI, No. 4.
Wedel, Theodore O., "The Body-Spirit Paradox of the Church," Vol. IV, No. 4.
———, "Evangelism's Threefold Witness: Kerygma, Koinonia, Diakonia," Vol. IX, No. 3.
West, Charles C., "The Obsolescence of History," Vol. XVII, No. 1.
Westphal, Charles, "The Marks of the Church," Vol. XII, No. 2.
Wickham, E. R., "Conversion in a Secular Age," Vol. XIX, No. 3.
Wight, Martin, "The Church, Russia, and the West," Vol. I, No. 1.
Wieser, Thomas, "Evangelism and the 'Death of God,'" Vol. XX, No. 2.
Wolf, Ernst, "Lost Unity?" Vol. I, No. 1.
Wolf, H. H., "Christ at Work in History," Vol. XVIII, No. 1.

INDEX